BIBLE STUDY COMMENTARY

Obadiah, Jonah

BRYAN BEYER · JOHN WALTON

Lamplighter Books Grand Rapids, Michigan
Zondervan Publishing House

OBADIAH, JONAH: BIBLE STUDY COMMENTARY
Jonah portion copyright © 1982 by John H. Walton
Obadiah portion copyright © 1988 by Bryan E. Beyer
All rights reserved.

Lamplighter Books are published by the Zondervan Publishing House
1415 Lake Drive, S.E., Grand Rapids, Michigan 49506

Library of Congress Cataloging-in-Publication Data

Beyer, Bryan E.
   Obadiah, Jonah / Bryan E. Beyer, John Walton.
      p. cm. – (Bible study commentary)
   "Lamplighter books."
   Bibliography: p.
   ISBN 0-310-36311-X
   1. Bible. O.T. Obadiah—Commentaries. 2. Bible. O.T. Jonah—Commentaries. I. Walton, John, 1952– . II. Title. III. Series: Bible study commentary series.
BS1595.3.B49   1988
224'.91077—dc 19   88–18700
                                                              CIP

Printed in the United States of America

88 89 90 91 92 93 / CH / 10 9 8 7 6 5 4 3 2 1

Obadiah

BRYAN BEYER

BOOKS IN THE BIBLE STUDY COMMENTARY SERIES

Genesis Leon J. Wood
Exodus F.B. Huey, Jr.
Leviticus Louis Goldberg
Numbers F.B. Huey, Jr.
Deuteronomy Louis Goldberg
Joshua Paul P. Enns
Judges Paul P. Enns
Ruth Paul P. Enns
1, 2 Samuel Howard F. Vos
*1, 2 Kings Howard F. Vos
1, 2 Chronicles Eugene H. Merrill
Ezra, Nehemiah, Esther Howard F. Vos
Job D. David Garland
*Psalms Ronald B. Allen
Proverbs Eldon Woodcock
Ecclesiastes Louis Goldberg
Song of Songs Edward M. Curtis
Isaiah D. David Garland
Jeremiah F.B. Huey, Jr.
Lamentations Dan G. Kent
Ezekiel Paul P. Enns
Daniel Leon J. Wood
Hosea D. David Garland
Joel Ronald B. Allen
Amos D. David Garland
Obadiah, Jonah John H. Walton and Bryan E. Beyer
Micah Jack R. Riggs
Nahum, Habakkuk, Zephaniah, Haggai J. N. Boo Heflin
Zechariah Homer Heater, Jr.
Malachi Charles D. Isbell
Matthew Howard F. Vos
Mark Howard F. Vos
Luke Virtus E. Gideon
John Herschel H. Hobbs
Acts Curtis Vaughan
Romans Curtis Vaughan and Bruce Corley
1 Corinthians Curtis Vaughan and Thomas D. Lea
*2 Corinthians Aída Besançon Spencer, William David Spencer
Galatians Curtis Vaughan
Ephesians Curtis Vaughan
Philippians Howard F. Vos
Colossians and Philemon Curtis Vaughan
The Thessalonian Epistles John F. Walvoord
The Pastoral Epistles E. M. Blaiklock
Hebrews Leon Morris
James Curtis Vaughan
1, 2 Peter, Jude Curtis Vaughan and Thomas D. Lea
1, 2, 3 John Curtis Vaughan
Revelation Alan F. Johnson

*Not yet published as of this printing

Contents—Obadiah

Chapter 1

An Introduction to Obadiah and His Prophecy

A. Historical Background

The year 586 B.C. witnessed the downfall of the southern kingdom of Judah. The mighty Nebuchadnezzar, king of Babylon, captured Jerusalem, destroyed the city and its temple, and led the inhabitants into captivity. The Jewish state would not achieve independence again for over 2,500 years.

Jerusalem's fall, tragic as it was, was not without warning. Prophets such as Isaiah, Micah, and Jeremiah had vehemently denounced the nation's sins, urging the people to remember the Law of Moses[1] and the God who had made them what they were. But it was not to be. Rather, the nation learned—the hard way—the consequence of violating its agreement with God as His favored nation.

The defeat of Judah, then, was not the defeat of God. Rather, God had demonstrated His sovereignty over His people by judging them for their sin. The exile, moreover,

---

[1] The account of God's giving the Law through Moses begins at Exod. 19:1. The Law was an important feature of the covenant, a divinely-initiated agreement wherein God graciously placed Himself in a special relationship to Israel. Israel's responsibility was to demonstrate her faithfulness to God by obedience to the covenant. Obedience would result in blessing to the nation; disobedience would result in judgment.

proved that God was in control of history, for He alone had predicted Judah's fall to the Babylonians (Isa. 41:21–29).

But God's sovereignty extended far beyond the borders of Israel and Judah. God had used Assyria to judge the northern kingdom of Israel (2 Kings 17:7–18); now He had used Babylon to judge Judah (2 Kings 24:1–3). God was indeed Lord of *all* nations, whether those nations recognized that fact or not.

The prophet Obadiah, ministering shortly after 586 B.C., announced God's judgment against the nation of Edom. Located directly south of the Dead Sea, the Edomites were the descendants of Esau, Jacob's brother (Gen. 25:19–26; 36:1). But despite this close blood relationship with Israel and Judah (Jacob's descendants), Edom became a bitter enemy of God's people and rejoiced when Jerusalem fell to Nebuchadnezzar's armies (Obad. 10–14; Ps. 137:7). Obadiah announced that God had not forgotten Edom, and would soon judge her iniquities, too.

B. Obadiah the Man

The book of Obadiah reveals nothing about the prophet besides his name, which means "servant of the Lord." Twelve different men of Scripture bear the name Obadiah, though none may be positively identified as the prophet. A rabbinic source suggests King Ahab's steward (1 Kings 18:3) is the Obadiah in question, but this suggestion lacks any supporting evidence.

C. Authorship and Date of the Book

Although the book of Obadiah does not specifically designate Obadiah as the author, it is likely he wrote the book that bears his name. Perhaps, after presenting his prophecy orally to encourage his own people, he committed his words to writing so that later generations could testify to the fulfillment of God's promises.

The date of the book of Obadiah has been the subject

of much discussion and debate among Bible scholars. Some interpreters date Obadiah around the year 850 B.C., while others date the book after 586 B.C., when Jerusalem fell to Babylon's forces. While arguments on either side are not definitive,[2] the book's internal evidence seems to favor the later date. Obadiah 10–14 describes Edom's gloating over a catastrophe that befell Jerusalem, and the language used appears too strong to refer to anything other than Jerusalem's fall. Some scholars have argued that Jeremiah borrowed from Obadiah's words, and that therefore Obadiah must be earlier, but the literary connections, even if certain, do not conclusively demonstrate borrowing from Obadiah.[3]

D. Purpose of the Book of Obadiah

The book of Obadiah announces judgment against Edom. Many people of Judah probably wondered about the future. What about God's enemies? Were they to escape judgment? Would Edom, despite its arrogance, miss punishment? Obadiah assures his audience: God has not forgotten Edom! Rather, the day will come when the people of Edom will feel the full force of God's wrath. The certainty of Edom's judgment no doubt brought hope to many Judeans, for coupled to Obadiah's prophecy of Edom's downfall was Obadiah's prophecy of Jacob's restoration.

E. Outline

I. Heading and Introduction (1)
II. Edom's Arrogance (2–4)
III. Edom's Coming Humiliation (5–9)

---

[2] See Leslie C. Allen, *Joel, Obadiah, Jonah, and Micah* (Grand Rapids: Wm. B. Eerdmans, 1976), pp. 129–133 for a complete discussion of the issues.

[3] Obad. 1b–5 is similar to Jer. 49:9,14–16. For a defense of the early date argument, see C.F. Keil and F. Delitzsch, *The Minor Prophets* (Grand Rapids: Wm. B. Eerdmans, 1978), pp. 339–349. Some scholars have suggested Obadiah borrowed from Jeremiah, or that the two cited a common source.

IV. Edom's Violence Toward Jacob (10–14)
V. The Day of the Lord (15–21)
   A. Against God's Enemies (15–16,18)
   B. For God and His People (17,19–21)

For Further Study

1. Read the story of Jacob and Esau in Gen. 25:19–27:45; 32:4–33:17 to discover some of the background behind the bitter enmity Obadiah describes.

2. What difference does it make if God is indeed Lord of *all* nations?

3. Look up "Edom" in a concordance or Bible encyclopedia.

Chapter 2

Interpretation of Obadiah

A. Heading and Introduction (1)

> The vision of Obadiah. This is what the Sovereign Lord says about Edom—

> We have heard a message from the Lord: an envoy was sent to the nations to say, "Rise, and let us go against her for battle."

The heading is brief and concise—"The vision of Obadiah." The writer gives none of his own credentials, though his contemporaries certainly knew him well (see Introduction). The word "vision" emphasizes that what we are about to read is not Obadiah's opinion, but God's revelation.

This revelatory aspect of the message is confirmed by the next phrase: "This is what the Sovereign Lord says about Edom." The prophet's role was that of a messenger; his message had its source in God, never in himself.

The nation of Edom lay directly south of the Dead Sea, right at Judah's southeast corner. The Edomites had descended from Esau, Jacob's brother (see Introduction), and the Bible records the struggles between these two progenitors (Gen. 25:19–34; 27:1–45). Later history witnessed the struggles continuing through the descendants of these men.[1] How tragic that two nations, so closely related by blood, should become such bitter enemies!

The second half of verse 1 reveals the means of God's judgment: earthly nations. Just as God had sovereignly used Assyria to judge the northern kingdom of Israel and Babylon to judge the southern kingdom of Judah, so He could and would use nations of earth to judge Edom. The envoy sent to the nations to gather them for battle may have some fulfillment in a literal person of history, but more likely is figurative language referring to the gathering of nations at the command of God. God will raise up powers hostile to Edom, and thereby fulfill His sovereign purpose.

B. Edom's Arrogance (2–4)

"See, I will make you small among the nations; you will be utterly despised.

The pride of your heart has deceived you, you who live in the clefts of the rocks and make your home on the heights, you who say to yourself, 'Who can bring me down to the ground?'

Though you soar like the eagle and make your nest among the stars, from there I will bring you down," declares the Lord.

A shift in speaker occurs in verse 2. Verse 1 closes with the nations' rallying cry against Edom: "Rise, and let us go against her for battle!" In verse 2, God speaks directly to Edom.

Verse 2 presents God's general announcement of judgment: "I will make you small among the nations." The Hebrew verb form here is usually translated in the past tense ("I made/have made you small"), but here emphasizes the certainty of Edom's destruction. The judgment is

---

[1]See e.g. Num. 20:14–21; 1 Sam. 14:47; 2 Sam. 8:14; 1 Kings 11:14–22; 2 Kings 8:20–22; 2 Chron. 20:1–23; 28:17; Amos 1:11–12.

so certain in God's sovereign plan that God speaks of it as though it were already a past event.

Verses 3–4 deal more specifically with one of Edom's most serious problems—pride. By exalting herself, Edom totally ignored the mighty hand of God.

Obadiah's description of the Edomites "who live in the clefts of the rocks" probably refers most directly to Sela, Edom's capital, located about fifty miles south of the Dead Sea.[2] Sela was built on a rocky, mountainous mass that extended almost a thousand feet into the sky. High, perpendicular rock walls surrounded the city on all but the southeast side, thus rendering it virtually impregnable and easy to defend. Edomites living in such an environment would certainly feel as if they were "soaring like the eagle" or "making their nest among the stars."

Edom's arrogance produced her defiant challenge: "Who can bring me down to the ground?" The challenge was really as much a statement as a question; Edom thought no one anywhere could destroy the kingdom she had built. But God answered Edom's challenge in verse 4b: "*I* will bring you down!" Edom's plans do not matter. Men may make plans and set goals, but God determines whether any of those goals ever become reality. By issuing such a challenge, Edom failed to consider that God is sovereign over *all* nations, and God had to remind Edom of this fact.

C. Edom's Coming Humiliation (5–9)

"If thieves came to you, if robbers in the night—Oh, what a disaster awaits you—would they not steal only as much as they wanted? If grape pickers came to you, would they not leave a few grapes? But how Edom will

---

[2] For more on this city and Edom in general see William H. Morton, "Umm el–Biyara," *Biblical Archeologist* 19 (1956), pp. 26–36, and "Edom," *Zondervan Pictorial Encyclopedia of the Bible*, v. 2 (Grand Rapids: Zondervan Publishing House, 1975), pp. 202–204.

be ransacked, his hidden treasures pillaged! All your allies will force you to the border; your friends will deceive you and overpower you; those who eat your bread will set a trap for you, but you will not detect it.

'In that day,' declares the Lord, 'will I not destroy the wise men from Edom, men of understanding in the mountains of Esau? Your warriors, O Teman, will be terrified, and everyone in Esau's mountains will be cut down in the slaughter.' "

In verses 2–4, Obadiah warned arrogant Edom in general terms of the judgment that lay ahead; God would bring her down. Now, in verses 5–9, the prophet describes more specifically the nature of that judgment. God may use human instruments to carry out His purpose, but the catastrophe that will befall Edom will be clearly recognizable as from His hand.

In verses 5–6, Obadiah demonstrated the severity of God's coming judgment against Edom by using two analogies from human experience. When a writer uses an analogy, he compares two items to show they are alike in some way; usually, he appeals to some fact his readers will readily accept. Then, the writer proceeds to argue that the two items are also alike in other ways. An analogy, then, is more an illustration than a logical argument; just because two items are similar in one way, it does not necessarily follow that they are alike in other ways. But it is precisely as illustrations that Obadiah's analogies add an important punch to his message. After reminding Edom how devastating and/or thorough human actions against another can be, he suggests God's judgment will prove even more devastating, more thorough, than anything Edom has ever seen. Everything—even the "hidden treasures"—will vanish.[3]

Obadiah's argument, simply stated, runs like this:

---

[3] The term "hidden treasures" may refer to the precious commodities the Edomites had stored high up in their rocky fortresses.

"Suppose for a minute that robbers came to plunder Edom's villages and countrysides. The damage would certainly be extensive, the personal loss great, and the unfortunate residents might need a long time to rebuild and recover their losses. But at least the robbers wouldn't steal everything. They would limit themselves to the more valuable items, and could only steal as much as they could successfully carry off. Not so with God; when the time of judgment comes, He will take everything. Or suppose grape gatherers harvested your grapes—naturally, they would try to be thorough, but would probably miss at least a few grapes in the process.[4] Not so with God—His judgment won't leave a trace of anything!"

In verse 7, Obadiah reveals another aspect of God's judgment against Edom: Edom's allies will betray her. The Hebrew expression translated by the NIV as "your allies" literally means "the men of your covenant." A covenant was an agreement between two parties in which each party bound itself to the other to perform certain duties or services; usually military alliances formed part of the agreement.[5] The prophet stresses that all of Edom's covenants with other nations will become worthless as the rulers not only fail to send assistance troops to Edom, but even join the attack themselves. The phrases "those who eat your bread" and "but you will not detect it" translate difficult Hebrew expressions. In the first phrase, "your bread" is all that appears in the Hebrew text, but the flow of the context suggests the NIV rendering. Two other possible translations for the second phrase are "there is no understanding in him" (that is, in Edom), and "there is no understanding in it" (that is, there is no comprehending the enemies' betrayal of Edom).[6] However one under-

---

[4] In Israel, harvesters were also to leave a portion of the harvest for the poor (Deut. 24:19–22) but we have no evidence that Edom maintained that practice.

[5] For more on God's covenant with Israel, see chapter 1, footnote 1.

[6] This latter sense seems to fit best the context, though one could understand

stands these two phrases, the thrust of the passage remains essentially the same: God will use those Edom thought were her friends to bring her down.

Verses 8–9 focus on yet another aspect of Edom's downfall: internal disintegration. Verse 8 is stated as a question, but we should understand it as purely rhetorical, expecting an affirmative answer. God will raise up armies to attack from without while simultaneously undermining the societal structure from within. The sovereign Lord specifically singles out for judgment two important elements of society: the wise and the warriors.

To function effectively, any society needs wise leadership. The words "wise men of Edom" do not refer merely to reflective philosophers, but rather to creative individuals whose discernment and guidance could successfully lead the nation. The Edomites apparently boasted many wise men and placed great confidence in them,[7] but God would remove their wisdom and render their words meaningless, thus destroying their effectiveness as leaders of society.

Solid military support also plays an important role in any society. In ancient times, if a country could not adequately assert itself and/or defend itself, it could quickly lose much of its territory and sometimes its independence.[8] Verse 9 describes the army's attitude: the men are terrified. As a result, "everyone in Esau's moun-

---

"there is no understanding in him" as a parenthetical thought about Edom. The NIV translation seems to be the least supportable on the basis of the Hebrew alone.

[7] Jer. 49:7 mockingly refers to this misplaced confidence. The book of Job, an important part of biblical wisdom literature, may have as its backdrop the land of Edom; cf. "Uz" in Job 1:1 and Lam. 4:21.

[8] This was often the case with Israel and its neighbors (1 Sam. 14:47; 2 Sam. 5:17–25; 8:1–14; 10:1–19; 1 Kings 11:14–25; 14:25–27; 15:16–22; 20:1–34; 22:1–38; 2 Kings 3:4–27; 6:8–7:16; 8:20–22, 28; 13:12, 20–25; 14:7–14, 25, 28; 15:19–20, 29, 37; 16:5–9; 17:3–6; 18:13–36; 23:31–35; 24:1–2, 8–17, 20–25:21).

tains will be cut down in the slaughter."[9] The terror may result from the army's realization that it now has no effective leaders (verse 8), or perhaps the Lord simply puts a spirit of terror and confusion within them (cf. 2 Kings 7:5–7). Either way, the result is the same: Edom, now lacking any kind of societal foundation, was certain to fall.

D. Edom's Violence Toward Jacob (10–14)

"Because of the violence against your brother Jacob, you will be covered with shame;[10] you will be destroyed forever. On the day you stood aloof while strangers carried off his wealth and foreigners entered his gates and cast lots for Jerusalem, you were like one of them.

You should not look down on your brother in the day of his misfortune, nor rejoice over the people of Judah in the day of their destruction, nor boast so much in the day of their trouble. You should not march through the gates of my people in the day of their disaster, nor look down on them in their calamity in the day of their disaster, nor seize their wealth in the day of their disaster. You should not wait at the crossroads to cut down their fugitives, nor hand over their survivors in the day of their trouble."

In verses 2–4, Obadiah has already pointed out one reason for Edom's coming judgment. Edom's pride had deceived her into thinking she was invincible, "soaring like the eagle" and "making her nest among the stars." God would humble Edom's proud spirit in the thorough manner described in verses 5–9. Edom would lose her

---

[9]The Edomites had descended from Esau, Jacob's brother (Gen. 25:19–26; 36:1). The word "Teman" likely refers to a specific city in Edom some scholars have located near Sela, Edom's capital; cf. Amos 1:12 and "Teman," *Zondervan Pictorial Encyclopedia of the Bible*, v. 5 (Grand Rapids: Zondervan Publishing House, 1978), pp. 621–622. "Teman" means "south," however, and others have understood the term in this more general sense as referring to all Edom (Jer. 49:7, 20).

[10]Literally means "shame will cover you."

property, her wise and understanding leadership, and her military might—everything on which she had built her society and placed her trust.

In verses 10–14, Obadiah presents a second reason behind Edom's judgment. Although Edom was Judah's closest relative,[11] she had not only refused to offer military assistance to Judah when the Babylonians invaded, but had even rejoiced in Judah's downfall (see also Ps. 137:7). Obadiah assures Edom that vengeance belongs to the Lord, and He will repay the Edomites for their treachery.

The prophet describes Edom's sin and imminent disgrace in verses 10 and 11. The Hebrew word translated as "violence" carries with it the connotation of injustice; that is, Edom's treatment of Jacob was not only harsh, but clearly immoral. The verdict against this atrocity was announced to Edom in verse 10b: "Shame will cover you."

Verse 11 relates Edom's standing aloof when catastrophe befell Judah. During the eighteen-month siege of Jerusalem by the armies of Babylon (Jer. 52:4–7), Edom offered Judah no assistance. When Nebuchadnezzar, king of Babylon, sent his leading officials into Jerusalem after the city fell (Jer. 39:1–3) Edom acted as "one of them," joining in the plundering and adding insult to injury.[12] And when Nebuzaradan, Nebuchadnezzar's captain of the guard, returned to Jerusalem a month later to destroy it (2 Kings 25:8–12), Edom roared its approval (Ps. 137:7). The reference to "casting lots over Jerusalem" reveals the means by which the victors divided the land among themselves. Lots provided an objective basis for apportioning the newly-acquired spoils.[13]

---

[11] The northern kingdom of Israel was a closer relative, but Assyria had taken Israel into captivity in 721 B.C., so Edom was the closest one left.

[12] The degree to which the Edomites actually entered Jerusalem is uncertain. Most likely much of their plundering of the Judeans occurred at the smaller towns in southern Judah, though verse 16 seems to indicate some direct contact with Jerusalem as well.

[13] These "spoils" could include not only land, but also property and people

Obadiah's perspective shifts somewhat as we move to verses 12–14. Whereas verses 10 and 11 declared Edom's violence against Judah during Jerusalem's siege and fall, verses 12–14 warn Edom concerning its behavior toward God's people in the immediate aftermath of this terrible destruction. The prophet announced eight prohibitions against Edom that fall into three categories: Edom's rejoicing over Judah's fall, Edom's plundering of Judah, and Edom's aggression against Judah's survivors.[14]

The first three prohibitions (verse 12) reveal a progression in Edom's pride. First, Edom looked upon its brother and took note of his distress. Second, Edom rejoiced over this distress. Third, Edom opened his mouth in great boasting,[15] as if to say, "What happened to Judah will never happen to me." Obadiah warns against such arrogance; God's judgment against Edom is soon to arrive!

Edom's confident arrogance of verse 12 led to his actions of verse 13. Again, we observe a progression: Edom entered the city gate, looked around and cast its eyes on the plunder, and stretched forth its hand to take it for its own. This plundering of Jerusalem and Judah no doubt followed on the heels of the Babylonian destruction, and was especially devastating; what little the Babylonians left, the Edomites took away.

But Edom's enmity with Judah did not end with stealing Judah's goods. Verse 14 shows Edom's hostility displayed itself in direct attacks against Judah's people. During the time of the Babylonian invasion, many Judeans

---

(see Josh. 19; Joel 3:3; Nah. 3:10; Matt. 27:35). For more information regarding lots and oracles in the Old Testament, see John Walton's comments in this volume, pages 19–29.

[14] The force of the Hebrew construction is stronger than the NIV suggests; instead of "You should not . . . " we should read "Don't! . . . " for each of the eight prohibitions of verses 12–14.

[15] The Hebrew of the third prohibition literally means "don't make great your mouth." For a similar expression see 1 Sam. 2:1; Ps. 35:21; Isa. 57:4.

tried unsuccessfully to flee the disaster;[16] those who did manage to escape probably had little besides the clothes on their backs. The Edomites had apparently positioned themselves at strategic points to prevent such escape attempts, and either killed the fleeing Judeans themselves or handed them over to the Babylonians.

These eight prohibitions demonstrate the intensity of Edom's hatred toward Judah. Edom had not simply ignored Judah's obvious need of assistance, but had itself become an aggressor. No such action could ever be justified, especially when such actions were directed against a brother (verse 10). In light of Judah's devastated condition, was there any hope of retribution? Could God's people ever expect to see Edom get its just reward? Obadiah answers these questions in the affirmative: Edom will fall, for the day of the Lord is coming.

E. The Day of the Lord (15–21)

"The day of the Lord is near for all nations. As you have done, it will be done to you; your deeds will return upon your own head. Just as you drank on my holy hill, so all the nations will drink continually; they will drink and drink and be as if they had never been. But on Mount Zion will be deliverance; it will be holy, and the house of Jacob will possess its inheritance. The house of Jacob will be a fire and the house of Joseph a flame; the house of Esau will be stubble, and they will set it on fire and consume it. There will be no survivors from the house of Esau. The Lord has spoken.

People from the Negev will occupy the mountains of Esau, and people from the foothills will possess the land of the Philistines. They will occupy the fields of Ephraim and Samaria, and Benjamin will possess Gilead. This company of Israelite exiles who are in

---

[16] Second Kings 25:4–7 records Zedekiah's unsuccessful attempt to escape with his army. See also Jer. 37:11–16, where Jeremiah was suspected of trying to desert to the enemy and was arrested.

Canaan will possess the land as far as Zarephath; the exiles from Jerusalem who are in Sepharad will possess the towns of the Negev. Deliverers will go up on Mount Zion to govern the mountains of Esau. And the kingdom will be the Lord's."

The expression "the day of Lord" occurs frequently in Old Testament prophecy, and the New Testament refines the concept even further. As the term implies, the day of the Lord is *the Lord's day*, when God enters into history in a special way to fulfill His holy purposes. Two basic features characterize the day of the Lord: judgment against God's enemies and the salvation of God's people.

As early as the eighth century B.C., Amos and Isaiah had spoken of the day of the Lord as drawing near and bringing judgment against sinful mankind. Isaiah saw in it the fall of Babylon (Isa. 13:6, 9); Amos declared judgment would also fall on God's own people, who failed to see their own sin (Amos 5:18–20). Later prophets shared these views; in the day of the Lord, God would judge sin everywhere, whether it was among the nations (Obad. 15) or among God's people (Joel 3:14; Zeph. 1:7–18). The prophet Ezekiel, writing in the early sixth century B.C., even commented that the day of the Lord was at least partially fulfilled when Jerusalem fell to the Babylonians (Ezek. 13:5).[17] The New Testament writers saw the day of the Lord as coming suddenly upon the unbelieving, sweeping them away to certain destruction (1 Thess. 5:2–3).

But the prophets also promised the day of the Lord would bring salvation to God's people. The judgment that fell on God's people would cleanse them and purify them for His purposes (Mal. 3:2–4). The hope of deliverance

---

[17]Ezekiel's prophetic call from God came in the year 592 (Ezek. 1:2–3); thus, his ministry overlapped with Obadiah's. The two men probably did not know each other, however, since Ezekiel prophesied as an exile in Babylon while Obadiah prophesied in Judah.

remained present for the faithful (Zeph. 2:1–3) as they looked to their sovereign Lord to pour out His Spirit and establish His kingdom (Joel 2:28–32). In the New Testament, the apostles wrote that the day of the Lord would feature not only the final destruction of evil (2 Thess. 2:1–2), but the salvation of believers, the creation of a new heaven and a new earth, and the establishment of God's everlasting kingdom (1 Thess. 5:4–11; 2 Peter 3:10–13).

In Obadiah 15–21, the prophet announces the day of the Lord will bring both judgment and salvation. God's judgment will fall upon all nations, and particularly upon Edom, but the same bell that tolls for Edom's demise will ring with peals of salvation for Israel and Judah.

1. Against God's Enemies (15–16, 18).

Although Obadiah begins this section by announcing that the day of the Lord is near "for all nations," his focus remains on Edom. The words "you" and "your" in verse 15 are in the singular, indicating that the prophet is specifically addressing Edom. Edom will receive its just recompense from God, who executes vengeance in full.

In verse 16, the subject and verb "you drank" shift to the plural forms in the Hebrew, and a question arises: whom is the prophet addressing? Since Obadiah always uses singular pronouns and verbs when he refers to Edom elsewhere in his book, some Bible interpreters have suggested that the prophet briefly addresses the Judeans in this verse. According to this understanding of the passage, Obadiah is comforting God's people with the assurance that just as they drank the cup of God's wrath, so the nations would receive the cup to drink, too.[18] While this interpretation is possible, Obadiah's alleged shift from

---

[18] Carl E. Armerding, *Expositor's Bible Commentary*, v. 7: *Daniel–Malachi* (Grand Rapids: Zondervan Publishing House, 1985), p. 353; Hans W. Wolff, *Obadiah and Jonah: A Commentary* (Minneapolis: Augsburg Publishing House, 1986), pp. 64–65.

Edom to Judah is far from clear, even in the original language. Since Obadiah has maintained Edom as the addressee throughout his prophecy, it seems more likely his plural subject and verb refer to individual Edomites who celebrated Judah's fall with carousing and revelry.[19] Obadiah promises that the day is coming when Edom, along with the other nations like her, will drink from a very different cup—the cup of God's wrath.

The expression "drink the cup" or similar variations appear quite often in the prophetic literature to describe the humiliating judgment God brings against various nations as He pours out His wrath against them (Isa. 51:17; Jer. 25:15,17; 51:7; Hab. 2:15–16).[20] Here, the nations receive judgment much worse than the judgment of Judah; they will drink and drink until they are no more.

Obadiah focuses specifically on Edom's judgment again in verse 18. He portrays God's people as instruments in God's hands, devouring Edom as fire devours stubble.[21] The term "house of Joseph" refers to the northern kingdom of Israel (1 Kings 11:28; Ezek. 37:16, 19; Amos 6:6), and affirms a reunited Israel established by God Himself. The word "survivors" is the same word translated as "survivors" in verse 14. Because Edom had handed over Judah's survivors to captivity and/or death, so will God destroy Edom's survivors—none will remain. The verdict is certain, for "the Lord has spoken" (Isa. 24:3; 25:8; 40:5). God's Word will stand, but Edom will fall.

2. For God and His People (17, 19–21).

In the closing verses of his book, Obadiah describes God's future plans for His people. The day of the Lord has

---

[19]C.F. Keil and F. Delitzsch, *The Minor Prophets* (Grand Rapids: Wm. B. Eerdmans, 1978), pp. 366–67.

[20]For a New Testament usage of this expression, see Matt. 26:39, 42.

[21]The metaphor of fire and stubble in reference to God's judgment is quite common (Isa. 5:24; 10:17; 30:30; Joel 2:5; Mal. 4:1).

brought judgment against the nations and cleansing to God's people. Now, the focus shifts to a future time when God will establish His kingdom and rule in a special way among and through His people. Obadiah presents a general description of this time in verse 17 and a more specific description in verses 19–21.

Mount Zion lies on the southwest edge of Jerusalem, and often appears in the Old Testament as a designation for the entire city (Ps. 2:6; 137:3; Isa. 2:3; 3:16; Lam. 1:17). Zion, formerly a place of judgment, now becomes a place of deliverance again.

Obadiah also promises that Israel ("the house of Jacob") will "possess its inheritance," that is, Israel will receive the territory promised her by God from ancient times.[22] Various problems throughout Israel's history had prevented her from assuming full control of her inheritance,[23] but now God will remove such problems.

Obadiah relates many specific details concerning Israel's restoration in verses 19–21. People of the Negev,[24] the southern region of Judah, will expand their territory into Edom. Since Edom has fallen under God's judgment, the land has become available for God's people.

Obadiah also prophesies that people from the foothills of Judah will possess former Philistine territory. The Philistines were ancient foes of Israel who lived in Judah along the Mediterranean coast. They fought against Saul, Israel's first king, and were victorious (1 Sam. 31:1–10), but David, Saul's successor and Israel's greatest king, subdued them (2 Sam. 5:17–25). After David's reign, the Philistines appear occasionally in biblical history in bat-

[22] It is somewhat difficult to define precisely what the territory was, since general designations are often given (Gen. 12:7; 26:3–4; 28:13–14) or the cities are unknown (Josh. 13–19). Obadiah also gives us a description of this territory in verses 19–21, but even here we may not draw the borders absolutely.

[23] The book of Judges indicates that the primary problem was a lack of faith on Israel's part to go in and take the land (Judg. 2:1–23).

[24] The term is also sometimes spelled "Negeb."

tles against Judah, with each side trying to achieve independence from or to assert dominance over the other (2 Kings 18:8; 2 Chron. 17:11; 21:16–7; 26:6–7). The Judean foothills (Hebrew *shephelah*), located between the Philistine coast and the Judean highlands and formerly a constant "battle zone" for Judah and the Philistines, are now to be blessed, as its residents not only dwell in security due to God's judgment of Philistia, but now freely expand into former Philistine territory.[25]

Thus far, Obadiah's description has revealed a southern and western expansion. The text now indicates that northern and eastern movements are also to be a part of God's restoration. The northern territories of Ephraim and Samaria, conquered by Assyria in 721 B.C. (2 Kings 17:1–6), again form part of Israel. The tribe of Benjamin, the smallest of the tribal territories (Josh. 18:11–28), will receive the region of Gilead, a rich, fertile area east of the Jordan River near the Sea of Galilee. God's promise to Jacob that his descendants would expand to the west, east, north, and south (Gen. 28:14) is now to be realized in its fullest sense.

Verse 20 brings together the exiles of the Assyrian captivity (721 B.C.) and the exiles of the Babylonian captivity (586 B.C.). Those in the north (Israel's former exiles) will possess the land as far north as Zarephath, a city located between Sidon and Tyre along the Mediterranean coast.[26] Jerusalem's former exiles, described here as "in Sepharad," will possess the cities of the Negev. Many modern scholars understand "Sepharad" as a reference to Sardis, ancient capital of Lydia in Asia Minor, though the identification must remain tentative.[27] The exiles now see

---

[25] The five major cities of the Philistines were Ashdod, Ashkelon, Gaza, Ekron, and Gath, all of which appear often in the Bible.

[26] Elijah the prophet ministered for a time at Zarephath (1 Kings 17:9, 10).

[27] *The Interpreter's Bible*, v. 6 (Nashville: Abingdon Press, 1956), p. 867; Leslie C. Allen, *The Books of Joel, Obadiah, Jonah and Micah* (Grand Rapids:

the day of God's restoration, and joyfully resettle the homeland God has prepared for them.

Obadiah's prophecy culminates in verse 21. Briefly, the prophet reiterates a theme he already introduced in verses 18–20: God's people will rule over the territory of Edom. The term "delivers" may refer to the army God uses to bring about His kingdom. Clearly, however, the kingdom will be the Lord's; He has ordained it, He will bring it about, and He will receive all the glory because of it. God is king already, but Obadiah looks ahead to a time when all the world will know, when every knee will bow to Him. The Christian looks for this kingdom, too, in the person of Jesus Christ, with whom he will one day reign (1 Cor. 6:2; 15:24–28; Rev. 5:9–10).

Many interpreters have tried to pinpoint the date of Edom's fall, the fulfillment of Obadiah's prophecy. The task has proven somewhat difficult, since the ancient sources available do not specifically record Edom's defeat. However, from certain biblical texts we may infer that Edom fell to Babylon shortly after Judah (Jer. 25:9, 21; Mal. 1:3). In later times, some Edomites occupied southern Judah, forming the region of Idumaea. The Idumaeans clashed with the Jews on several occasions during the Maccabean period (second century B.C.), but later came under Roman control as did the Jews. The loss of their independence was soon followed by their extermination; the last Idumaeans died defending Jerusalem against the Romans in A.D. 70.[28] The words of Obadiah became reality—"You will be destroyed forever."

Wm. B. Eerdmans, 1976), p. 171. C.F. Keil and F. Delitzsch, *The Minor Prophets*, pp. 373–374, argue the reference is to Sparta, the powerful ancient city of Greece.

[28] C.F. Keil and F. Delitzsch, *The Minor Prophets*, pp. 376–378; "Edom," *Zondervan Pictorial Encyclopedia of the Bible*, v. 2 (Grand Rapids: Zondervan Publishing House, 1975), p. 204.

For Further Reading

1. What did God think of Edom's pride? How can we avoid pride in our own lives?

2. Read through Obadiah to discover how the prophet uses figurative language. What are some of the images he uses to make his points?

3. Compare Obadiah 1–5 with Jeremiah 49:9, 14–16. Do you think prophets read each other's prophecies or ever preached similar messages?

4. How do you think you would feel if you were in Obadiah's situation? To further assist you in understanding how he must have felt, read the book of Lamentations and Psalm 137.

Bibliography

Allen, Leslie C. *The Books of Joel, Obadiah, Jonah and Micah.* Grand Rapids: Wm. B. Eerdmans, 1976.

Beitzel, Barry J. *The Moody Atlas of Bible Lands.* Chicago: Moody Press, 1985.

Bullock, C. Hassell. *An Introduction to the Old Testament Prophetic Books.* Chicago: Moody Press, 1986.

Buttrick, George A., ed. *The Interpreter's Bible*, v. 6. Nashville: Abingdon Press, 1956.

Craigie, Peter C. *Twelve Prophets*, v. 1. Philadelphia: Westminster Press, 1984.

Feinberg, Charles L. *The Minor Prophets.* Chicago: Moody Press, 1976.

Gaebelein, Frank E., ed. *The Expositor's Bible Commentary*, v. 7 (Daniel–Malachi). Grand Rapids: Zondervan Publishing House, 1985.

Hailey, Homer. *A Commentary on the Minor Prophets.* Grand Rapids: Baker Book House, 1972.

Harrison, R.K. "Edom," *Zondervan Pictorial Encyclopedia of the Bible* (Grand Rapids: Zondervan Publishing House, 1978), pp. 202–204.

Keil, C.F. and F. Delitzsch. *The Minor Prophets.* Grand Rapids: Wm. B. Eerdmans, 1978 (reprint).

Morton, William H. "Umm el-Biyara," *Biblical Archaeologist* 19 (1956), pp. 26–36.

Watts, John D. W. *Obadiah: A Critical Exegetical Commentary.* Grand Rapids: Wm. B. Eerdmans, 1969.

Wolff, Hans W. *Obadiah and Jonah: A Commentary.* Minneapolis: Augsburg Publishing House, 1986.

Young, F. E. "Teman," *Zondervan Pictorial Encyclopedia of the Bible*, v. 5 (Grand Rapids: Zondervan Publishing House, 1978), pp. 621–622.

Jonah

JOHN WALTON

BOOKS IN THE BIBLE STUDY COMMENTARY SERIES

Genesis Leon J. Wood
Exodus F.B. Huey, Jr.
Leviticus Louis Goldberg
Numbers F.B. Huey, Jr.
Deuteronomy Louis Goldberg
Joshua Paul P. Enns
Judges Paul P. Enns
Ruth Paul P. Enns
1, 2 Samuel Howard F. Vos
*1, 2 Kings Howard F. Vos
1, 2 Chronicles Eugene H. Merrill
Ezra, Nehemiah, Esther Howard F. Vos
Job D. David Garland
*Psalms Ronald B. Allen
Proverbs Eldon Woodcock
Ecclesiastes Louis Goldberg
Song of Songs Edward M. Curtis
Isaiah D. David Garland
Jeremiah F.B. Huey, Jr.
Lamentations Dan G. Kent
Ezekiel Paul P. Enns
Daniel Leon J. Wood
Hosea D. David Garland
Joel Ronald B. Allen
Amos D. David Garland
Obadiah, Jonah John H. Walton and Bryan E. Beyer
Micah Jack R. Riggs
Nahum, Habakkuk, Zephaniah, Haggai J. N. Boo Heflin
Zechariah Homer Heater, Jr.
Malachi Charles D. Isbell
Matthew Howard F. Vos
Mark Howard F. Vos
Luke Virtus E. Gideon
John Herschel H. Hobbs
Acts Curtis Vaughan
Romans Curtis Vaughan and Bruce Corley
1 Corinthians Curtis Vaughan and Thomas D. Lea
*2 Corinthians Aída Besançon Spencer, William David Spencer
Galatians Curtis Vaughan
Ephesians Curtis Vaughan
Philippians Howard F. Vos
Colossians and Philemon Curtis Vaughan
The Thessalonian Epistles John F. Walvoord
The Pastoral Epistles E. M. Blaiklock
Hebrews Leon Morris
James Curtis Vaughan
1, 2 Peter, Jude Curtis Vaughan and Thomas D. Lea
1, 2, 3 John Curtis Vaughan
Revelation Alan F. Johnson

*Not yet published as of this printing

To the
College and career
Sunday school class
of 1981
at
Faith Bible Church
Montgomery, Ohio

Contents—Jonah

List of Abbreviations

ANET   J. Pritchard (ed.), *Ancient Near Eastern Texts*, Princeton, 1969.

BWL   W. G. Lambert, *Babylonian Wisdom Literature*, Oxford, 1960.

CAD   A. L. Oppenheim *et al.* (eds.), *The Assyrian Dictionary of the Oriental Institute of the University of Chicago*, Chicago, 1956—.

HTR   *Harvard Theological Review*

KJV   *King James Version*

NASB   *New American Standard Bible*

NIV   *New International Version*

TB   *Tyndale Bulletin*

VT Supp   *Vetus Testamentum Supplement*

Introduction

Most biblical commentaries begin by introducing the reader to some of the background of the book under consideration. This is normally a logical procedure in that much of the verse-by-verse analysis and interpretation can be influenced by information such as date, authorship, and purpose of the book.

Jonah, however, is one of those few biblical books in which the introductory issues are so difficult and controversial that they can be settled only *on the basis of* the verse-by-verse analysis and interpretation. For this reason, we have chosen to adopt the unusual procedure of dealing with the "introductory matters" at the end—after we have analyzed the text.

Of course, there are a few facts that are not a matter of controversy and that would be helpful for forming a foundation. Outside of the Book of Jonah, the prophet is referred to only once in the Old Testament (2 Kings 14:25). This reference enables us to connect him with the reign of Jeroboam II, king of Israel, who reigned from 793–753 B.C. This, then, places Jonah just after the time of Elisha, and immediately prior to the beginning of the great era of prophecy that began with Amos, Hosea, and Isaiah. It was a time of unparalleled prosperity in both Israel and Judah. We will deal more with these matters in chapter 5.

Chapters 1–4 contain the textual analysis along with our own translation, passage by passage. Several of the interpretations presented differ in varying degrees from past interpretations. In such cases I have attempted to present the evidence as fully as possible and to include a fair evaluation of the major views of the past. It is hoped that this will provide opportunity for maximum interaction with the text whether in group discussion or in personal Bible study.

Outline

I. Jonah's Flight (1:1–17)
   A. Jonah's call (1:1–2)
   B. The ship, the storm, and the sailors (1:3–16)
   C. The great fish (1:17)
II. Jonah's Prayer and Deliverance (2:1–10)
III. In Nineveh (3:1–10)
   A. The city of Nineveh (3:1–3)
   B. The message of Jonah (3:4)
   C. The response of the Ninevites (3:5–9)
   D. God's mercy (3:10)
IV. Jonah's Lesson (4:1–11)
   A. Jonah's complaint (4:1–4)
   B. The object lesson: the vine and the parasite (4:5–8)
   C. The application (4:9–11)

Chapter 1

Jonah's Flight
(Jonah 1:1–17)

A. Jonah's Call (1:1–2)

> The instructions of the LORD[1] came to Jonah, son of Amittai saying: "Arise, go to the great city Nineveh and denounce it, for its wickedness has come to my attention."

We have translated the first phrase of the book as "the instructions of the LORD" rather than the more common translation, "the word of the LORD" in order to differentiate between the phrase used here (and also in Jer. 1:4 and Hos. 1:2) and the phrase that is very similar and that is used to introduce the majority of the prophetic books (Hos. 1:1; Joel 1:1; Mic. 1:1; Zeph. 1:1; Hag. 1:1; Zech. 1:1; Mal. 1:1). In all of these books the "word of the LORD" refers to the message that the prophet was presenting to his audience in the name of the LORD. Jonah 1:1 and the rest of this type, on the other hand, present instructions given by the LORD to His prophet.[2]

---

[1]The translation "LORD" has been used throughout in both text and commentary to designate the personal name of the Israelite God which occurs in the Hebrew text as YHWH. The reader should understand that while the term "God" is a generic term that can apply to any gods, YHWH is a personal name and refers specifically to Israel's God. Thus it is YHWH ("the LORD") who speaks to Jonah, but the Ninevites believe God. The commentary will occasionally point out significant reasons why one or the other is used.

[2]Cf. also 1 Samuel 15:10; 2 Samuel 7:4; 1 Kings 6:11; 16:1; 17:2, 8; 21:17, 28; Isaiah 38:4; and many instances in Jeremiah and Ezekiel.

In what way, we might ask, did these instructions come to Jonah? Was there an audible voice or was it perhaps just a suggestion that came to him with such forcefulness that it could not be ignored? The text says nothing of the LORD or the angel of the LORD appearing to Jonah.

A hint may be found in verse 3, where it is stated that it was from the "presence of the LORD" (KJV, NASB) that Jonah fled. An examination of this Hebrew phrase *(milliphnē)* shows that it was used when a person came out of an official audience with the king. For example, Joseph went out "from the presence of" Pharaoh into the entire land of Egypt (Gen. 41:46), and a messenger came "from the presence of" the king of Israel to take Elisha prisoner (2 Kings 6:32). There are also examples of official audience with a prophet (2 Kings 5:27) and with the LORD (Cain, Gen. 4:16). Items such as the altar and the ark of the covenant are said to be in "the presence of" the LORD (Lev. 10:2; 16:12; Num. 16:46; 17:9; 20:9).

The Hebrew phrase as it is used in Jonah cannot merely signify that Jonah was running away from the LORD, for were that the case, a different Hebrew term *(mippnē)* would be used.[3] The implication, then, is that these instructions came to Jonah in an official audience with the LORD, though the LORD may have been represented merely by His voice.

The reason behind Jonah's mission was that the wickedness of Nineveh had come to the LORD's attention. This, of course, does not imply that the LORD had been previously unaware of this great city's depravity, but rather, that the situation had so degenerated that even His great mercy and patience had at last been overshadowed by the mandate of justice. In this, the case of Nineveh was similar to that of Sodom and Gomorrah (Gen. 18–19). God tempers His behavioral expectations of man in proportion to the degree to which He has revealed Himself and His will to man. Thus the conditions in Sodom or Nineveh

---

[3]Genesis 16:6, 8; 35:1, 7; Exodus 2:15; Judges 11:3; 1 Samuel 21:10; 1 Kings 2:7; 12:2.

would have to be far worse to warrant God's judgment than they would have to be in Jerusalem or Samaria. On an individual level, this might be compared to the idea that God is not as interested in where we are spiritually, as He is in how far we have come.[4]

B. The Ship, the Storm, and the Sailors (1:3–16)

But Jonah arose to flee to Tarshish from the audience with the LORD. So he went down to Joppa, located a ship going to Tarshish, paid the fare and boarded her to go with them to Tarshish away from the audience with the LORD. But the LORD hurled a great wind into the sea and there was such a great storm in the sea that the ship was about to break up. And the sailors were afraid and each cried out to his god; and they jettisoned the ship's cargo into the sea to lighten themselves. Now Jonah had gone down into the hold and laid down and slumbered. But the first mate approached him and said, "What are you doing sleeping? Get up and cry out to your god, perhaps that god will concern himself with us and we will not perish." And they said among themselves, "Come, let us cast lots so that we might discover on whose account this catastrophe has befallen us." So they cast lots, and the lot fell on Jonah. So they said to him, "Tell us now, on whose account this catastrophe has befallen us. What is your occupation? Where are you coming from? What is your nationality? Where are your kin from?" And he said to them, "I am a Hebrew and it is the LORD, the God of heaven whom I serve, who made the sea and the dry land." Now the men grew very fearful and they said to him, "What is this you have done?" (for the men knew that it was from an audience with the LORD that he was fleeing because he had told them). So they said to him, "What shall we do to you in order that the sea may calm down for us?" (for the sea was getting stormier). And he said to them, "Pick me up and throw me overboard so that the sea may be calm for you, because I (now) know that it is on my account that this great storm is upon you." But the men rowed to reach the shore, but

---

[4]Luke 12:47–48. Cf. C. S. Lewis, *Mere Christianity* (New York: Macmillan, 1960), pp. 177–83.

they did not succeed, for the sea was growing stormier about them. And they implored the LORD and they said, "Please LORD, do not let us perish for the life of this man, and do not charge us with shedding innocent blood; for you, O LORD, have done as you have pleased." Then they picked up Jonah and threw him overboard, and the sea stopped its raging. Then the men were in great awe of the LORD and they offered a sacrifice to the LORD and made vows.

Jonah at once determined that he did not want to obey the instructions given to him by the LORD, so he immediately took steps to avoid another audience. The one who was given instructions in official audience had a task to perform and would do so as the personal representative of the royal personage by whom he was commissioned (cf. Gen. 41:46 and 2 Kings 6:32). Thus it was this commission (which had been given in divine audience) from which Jonah was fleeing. Jonah's intent was not necessarily to go the opposite direction, but to get away far and fast. He did not think for an instant that either distance or speed would put him out of the range of the LORD'S reach (for we have seen that that sort of flight would be expressed in a different way in Hebrew). Did Jonah not know that the LORD would not be refused? Yes he knew that in theory, but just as many do even today, he still fled. "Perhaps," he may have thought, "if I am stubborn or make recruitment too difficult, the LORD will just find someone else for the job." The LORD'S tenacity, however, was soon to be demonstrated.

Jonah proceeded to Joppa and boarded a ship bound for Tarshish, whose location is unknown. The most common identification has been Tartessus, on the southern coast of Spain. There is very little evidence, however, to support this conclusion.

The phrase, "ships of Tarshish" (1 Kings 10:22; Isa. 23:1; etc.), refers to merchant ships, so it must have been a trading port. The meaning of the name Tarshish has led others to suggest that it was a place for the smelting of ore. All of these suggestions offer possibilities, but there is no sufficient evidence to bolster the argument. Tarshish could just be the farthest port imaginable. In English we might say that he headed for Timbuktu!

The Phoenicians were by and large responsible for most of the sea traffic in the Mediterranean during the first half of the first millennium B.C. It was they who pioneered exploration and trade by sea. It is therefore altogether likely that Jonah found himself on board a Phoenician vessel.

Once out to sea, the vessel encountered such a ferocious storm that even the seasoned seamen quailed with fear. Their first response was that each man cried out to his god. Many of the sailors could have been Phoenician, but many other peoples could have been represented both among crew and passengers. Such an ethnic mix would, of course, mean that each worshiped a different set of gods. Phoenicians or Canaanites may have worshiped Baal, Hadad, or Anat; Assyrians could have been worshipers of Assur, Ishtar, Ninurta, or Shamash; Babylonians would serve perhaps Marduk or Nabu. Furthermore, in Mesopotamia there was an entire hierarchy of protecting spirits, patron deities, lower eschelon gods and goddesses and senior members of the Pantheon. An individual worshiper would not have the right connections to approach the chief deity, Marduk, directly. He would have to go through divine channels. The statement, then, that each called on his own god, could refer not only to the fact that various religious groups were represented, but could also suggest that they were invoking their patron or family level deities, who would in turn make request to their divine superiors, eventually bringing the matter before the god who had been responsible for the storm or who had been offended.

The attention of the sailors to the religious aspects of the situation did not mean they neglected the practical aspects of their training, and the cargo was duly jettisoned.

By now the reader may wonder how Jonah was responding to all of this. We are informed that Jonah had gone below deck and had fallen asleep, apparently before the storm had begun. The word used here (v. 5) for ship is different from that used through-

out the passage. Many commentators have noticed that the word
used here is cognate to the normal word for ship in Aramaic or
Arabic. We should also note, however, that the word has a very
suitable Akkadian cognate[5] which would give a preferable
meaning. We will later see that Aramaic-type vocabulary is often
given as a reason for a late dating of the Book of Jonah. In this
instance, we can see that the influence need not have been
Aramaic.

As Jonah slumbered down in the hold, he was rousted out by a
gentleman in authority whom we have designated the "first
mate." "Chief Petty Officer" may be an alternative. In the text
he appears to be named captain of the crew. The ironical twist of
this pagan seaman telling an Israelite prophet that he ought to
be praying has not escaped the notice of commentators. In this
we are reminded of the rebuke that Abraham received on two
different occasions from pagan kings for attempting to pass his
wife off as his sister (Gen. 12:18; 20:9–10). The first mate urged
Jonah to get up and pray to his god with the hope that "perhaps
that god will concern himself with us and we will not perish."
The concept here is clear. The sailors figured that the more gods
they could make contact with, the better chance they had of
getting through to one who could do something about their
plight. After all, they did not know which god was responsible
for the storm. They sought a god who would take their case into
the court of the gods and present a defense on their behalf—
thus, a god who would "concern himself" with them. The word
that we have translated as "to concern himself" is seemingly an
Aramaic word. In the Bible the root is used only in the Aramaic
portion of the Book of Daniel (Dan. 6:4) and has the meaning "to
plan, think." In Jonah it is reflexive/passive, thus our translation.

In verse 7 we read that the sailors determined to cast lots in
order to discover "on whose account" the storm had come. We
ought first to ask whether they were seeking who was the cause

---

[5]*Sapannu*=lower parts; e.g. "in the lower parts of the sea."

(i.e., a god), or who was at fault (i.e., the individual). An easy solution is found in verse 12 where Jonah used the same language to confess his complication in the matter. We can therefore see that the sailors sought the individual whose offense had brought on the storm. The second question is what role lots had in determining who was at fault. The natural inclination, and the unanimous suggestion of commentators has been the explanation that the one on whom the lot fell was the guilty party. The difficulty here is that in verse 8, after the lot fell on Jonah, the sailors turned to him and asked, "On whose account has this calamity befallen us?" Commentators variously try to circumvent this problem by deleting the question of verse 8 (though principles of textual criticism would support its retension), or by revising it so that it asks a different question (totally unsupported by the Hebrew), or by interpreting around it by suggesting that the sailors wanted (or needed) Jonah to confirm the outcome of the lots. All of these textual gymnastics are necessary only if we assume that lots indicated the guilty party. Let us take a moment to look more closely at the evidence for such an assumption.

Excursus: Lots and Oracles in the Old Testament

Lots are mentioned frequently, and in their most basic sense they were considered an objective means by which to make a decision or a division. Canaan was divided among the Israelites by lot and the duties of each tribe for temple service were assigned by lot. In this way it is similar to our practice of drawing straws. In the prophets the word took on the meaning of "destiny" or "fate." Proverbs 16:33 makes it clear that the decision brought about by the lot was God's will, but this is only a statement of God's sovereignty. People using the lot were not seeking an answer from God (i.e., an oracle), they were only seeking objectivity.

The casting of lots is frequently referred to by commentators as the means by which a guilty or chosen person could be indicated. This bears examination.

Joshua 7:14–18. In seeking to determine the identity of the party who violated the ban, Joshua follows a carefully explained procedure. The entire group under consideration "draws near" and the LORD "takes" one from the group. The procedure was one of gradual narrowing: one tribe was "taken" from the twelve, one clan from the tribe, one household from the clan, one individual from the household. Once Achan was "taken" there was no longer any question of his guilt. Joshua did not ask him to confirm the choice, but asked, "What have you done?" Guilt was certain, only the details were needed. The word for lots is never mentioned in this passage.

1 Samuel 14:40–42. In this incident, the procedure of tribe-clan-household-individual was not followed. Presumably the issue first addressed was whether the guilty party was among the army at large or the leadership (Saul and Jonathan). The choice here is always between two. The first round was between the army and the generals, the second between Saul and Jonathan. Again they "draw near" and the guilty party was "taken." As in Joshua, lots are not mentioned (though some translations add it). If the Septuagint reading of this passage is correct, however, Urim and Thummim are mentioned. These will be discussed in the section dealing with oracles.

1 Samuel 10:20–21. In this passage it was not guilt that was being indicated; rather, the people were seeking to appoint a king. It would seem unusual that they would use an objective means such as lots to make such a decision. In fact, the same procedure was used as in Joshua 7, and again, no lots are mentioned. We would expect that in such a case, an oracle would be asked.

Oracles used various mechanisms, but the purpose was always the same: to discover the will of God. The procedure was to ask a yes/no question and expect the deity to manipulate the oracular device so as to give his answer. The Urim and Thummim, though enigmatic, were clearly oracular in nature. They were part of the priestly paraphernalia (Exod. 28:30; Lev. 8:8; Deut. 33:8; Ezra 2:63; Neh. 7:65), and were specified as being consulted for oracles (Num. 27:21; 1 Sam. 28:6). It has often been suggested that Urim and Thummim involved the casting of lots, but in 1 Samuel 28:6, the Urim failed to give an answer. Such could not occur with normal lots.

Oracles in general were an accepted means of establishing the will of God in the Old Testament. They were not included in the divination practices outlawed in Deuteronomy 18:9–13. In the Ancient Near East, omens were frequently used as oracular devices. Omens were, however, included in the category of divination and the reading of them was unlawful in Israel. Astrology and the reading of tea leaves are present-day uses of omens. In ancient days the most popular type of omen derived from the configurations of the entrails of sacrificial animals. Certain configurations were considered favorable while others were considered unfavorable. These readings could easily be used for oracles by interpreting a favorable configuration as a yes answer to a specific question while an unfavorable configuration would constitute a no answer. The basic difference between oracles and omens was that omens did not need to have anything to do with deity—they merely gave knowledge of the future. Oracles were by nature deistic—they sought the will or pleasure of the god. In the Ancient Near East the two were intertwined. In Israel, omens were outlawed while oracles, using acceptable devices, were allowed. There are several examples of oracles being asked in the Old Testament, though they have not often been recognized as oracles. We will now examine these.

1 Samuel 6:7–12. In this incident, the Philistines determined that if the God of Israel was responsible for their difficulties, they had better seek to placate Him. However, they did not want to humiliate themselves (by acknowledging the superiority of the God of their conquered peoples) if He was not responsible. They therefore conceived of their experiment. The (oracular) question they asked was indirectly put to the Israelite God: Are You responsible for our sufferings? The answer was determined by setting up a situation where one of two things could happen: a) If the answer was no, natural laws would remain intact and the two cows would turn right around and head for their crying calves in the barn to both meet the needs of the calves and to relieve their own bulging udders; b) If the answer was yes, events would go against all natural expectations and the two cows, which had never pulled a cart (and therefore knew nothing of staying on a road), would ignore their pleading calves and bulging udders and would, unprodded, trot merrily down the path, straight for the Israelite Beth Shemesh. The oracle, for such it was, required divine manipulation of natural laws in order to be answered in the affirmative. On the other hand, a no answer was no answer at all and would leave the issue unsettled.

Genesis 24:12–14. Abraham's servant, faced with the difficult task of choosing a bride for Isaac, likewise used the means at his disposal for consulting God by oracle. In this instance again, one of two things could happen: a) If the answer was no, natural expectations would be realized—the servant would ask for a drink and be given one; b) If it was yes, events would go against all logic, indeed, against all sanity, and the girl, upon being asked for a drink of water, would offer to draw water for his entire caravan of camels. Surely this constituted divine manipulation! The positive response went against all natural laws of human behavior: No one in their right mind would make such an offer. A no answer would again have left the situation unresolved —the question would have remained.

Judges 6:36–40. In this familiar incident there is an unusual reversal for which, we expect, there must be good reason. Gideon, as with the Philistines and Abraham's servant, set up a situation in which one of two things could happen: a) In this setup, if the answer was yes, natural laws would remain intact. It was recognized long ago[6] that for the fleece to be wet while the rock threshing floor was dry was not unusual. Wool is very absorbent and can retain water for a long time, while any dew that had fallen on the rock would quickly evaporate when the sun rose. b) Here, the "no" alternative is not stated, though we would have to assume that it would have represented a deviation

---

[6]C. F. Birney, *Judges* (New York: 1970), p. 204.

from natural expectation. In regard to the switch (i.e., yes-natural, no-unnatural), we might suggest that it was occasioned by the fact that Gideon had already been told the answer to the question that he was asking (v. 37) and he was, in a sense, giving the Lord one last chance to back out. If the Lord was going to change His mind (and now say "no, do not go"), then the oracular "device" would have to be manipulated by God to say no, not yes.

Unlike the previous passages, the expected natural occurrence took place here. The fleece was wet and the rock was dry. From an oracular standpoint, this left the issue unresolved and the question unanswered. In Gideon's case it left his former instructions unaltered. We can now understand Gideon's hesitance to proceed with the process as he did. At last, however, he overcame his timidity and with profuse apology (v. 39) he reversed the indicators, resorting to normal oracular procedure. He wanted the Lord to tell him again to go, this time by oracle, just to make sure that he had gotten the message straight. Therefore, in verse 39 we see the familiar alternatives: a) If no, the normal should occur; b) if yes, events would go against all expectations.[7]

The possible bridge between lots and oracles was the Urim and Thummim. Lots were intended to be objective. They assumed that the laws of chance were in operation. Oracles, on the other hand, assumed divine manipulation of natural laws. If the Urim and Thummim was some type of lot, we would expect that where they were used oracularly, the determination made by them would have to go against all laws of chance.

---

[7]Lest we neglect this popular question, what role does "laying out the fleece" have today? Since the fleece was used as an oracle, we can see that this, as well as other examples of oracles, was a means of revelation sanctioned by God. From the time of David on, however, we do not see this type of oracle used anymore. Questions about the will of God were asked of the prophets, through whom God revealed Himself. The use of the prophets for divine revelation was replaced, in turn, by the written Word of God, the Bible. "Laying out the fleece" and other uses of oracular device were only a temporary means by which God could reveal Himself. Today we have a more complete, written revelation to direct us in His will.

The "choice of the guilty/favored person" passages discussed above would appear to demand an oracle as opposed to a casting of lots. Objectivity would not be desirable. Again, it would seem that if a lot-casting device were used, it would be used oracularly; i.e., the answer would somehow have to go against the odds. This brings us back to our consideration of Jonah.

If, as we have suggested above, the casting of lots is not attested as a means of determining the guilty/chosen person, we then need an alternate explanation for the events as we find them in Jonah 1:7–8. Since the sailors were probably non-Israelite, it could be suggested that their use of lots differed from the use attested in Israel. A survey of the uses of lots in Mesopotamia shows no evidence of lots being used in cultic or oracular situations.[8] As in Israel, they were used for assigning shares of an estate, assigning shares of temple income to sanctuary officials, and for selection of the official of the year (eponym or limmu). Only in the practice of the Hittites is there any example of lots being used for divination.

Rather than go against the text with no cultural evidence to support the reconstruction, we should ask what the sailors expected the lots to tell them, if not who the guilty person was? Can the text make sense as it stands, with the sailors asking Jonah who was responsible for the calamity after the lot had fallen on him?

The repeated question, "whose fault is this storm?" (v. 8) could indicate that the lots were expected to help them to determine either a) who knew who was at fault for the storm, or b) who first reported the sin he might have committed that would incur the wrath of his god. In our estimation, the latter is the more probable. Remember that lots were not always used to pick one out of a group, but were used frequently to determine order within the group. When the temple duties were assigned, the lots were cast not to pick who would do them, but to deter-

---

[8]A. Leo Oppenheim, *Ancient Mesopotamia* (Chicago: University of Chicago Press, 1977), pp. 206–27.

mine which tribes would serve which months. It established an order (Neh. 10:34). When the land of Canaan was divided among the tribes, the lots were possibly used to determine who chose first, second, etc. (Josh. 18:10–19:51). In Jonah each of the sailors had their own god(s). In Canaanite and Mesopotamian religions, the individual was often unaware of what his particular offense may have been, or what act could have so incensed his god. The presence of an offense would be clear only because of the punishment or suffering. Inversely, the presence of suffering or anything deemed punishment would automatically imply that offense had taken place. The individual in such a situation would have to reach back into his recent or distant past to think of how he might have offended his god.[9] This seems to us a reasonable explanation of what was going on here in Jonah. The lot was cast in order to determine which individual told first of what offense he (or his people, or his family, or his king, etc.) may have committed to bring on the wrath of his god. Then the lot would be cast again and the next would tell his tale. Once all of the possibilities were before them, perhaps they could take more intelligent action toward appeasing the offended deity.

This now makes better sense of the questions of verse 8. How is the person employed? Where did he board the ship? What is his nationality? Where are his kin from? These questions were all intended to help Jonah think of possible connections to some offense. Was his employer involved in illegal operations? Had his family neglected their cultic duties? Had his king defied the priesthood? Did he get into any trouble at the last port? They wanted to explore all of the avenues.

Jonah's response was short and to the point. He first identified himself as a Hebrew. This would have answered several of their questions, but for Jonah it served as an introduction to what follows. "It is the LORD, the God of Heaven whom I serve, who made the sea and the dry land." Now the sailors became very fearful. Their method had been more effective than they ever

---

[9] Cf. ANET 391b, 392a, and 384b.

dreamed. Jonah served a god who was thought to have created the sea and the dry land—that's precisely the type of god who would be responsible for their plight! Furthermore, they were aware that Jonah was fleeing from this god.

The way in which the text presents the fact that the sailors knew that Jonah was fleeing from his God in verse 10 is very unusual. When had Jonah told them? If he told them right after his speech in verse 9, why does the text not just quote another line of Jonah's speech to include that? We would rather suspect that Jonah had mentioned this fact in passing before the storm, and that their great fear at this point in the account derived from their having put two and two together. The fact that Jonah was fleeing from audience with his god would not necessarily have had anything to do with the storm in most cases. Without having the information about who Jonah's God was, the flight from that God portended no consequences for the sailors. But now the sailors would be greatly distressed: "You didn't tell us that this god *made the sea!*" (after all, He could have been the god of bricks or of grain or of scribes, or any number of other things). This was just cause for fear.

The casting of further lots to hear other tales was now unnecessary. The sailors had only to ask, "What shall we do to you?" We again might ask, what answer did the sailors expect to this question? From verse 13 we might assume that they expected Jonah to tell them to take him back to his starting point—for this is indeed what they attempted to do. Whatever options may have existed, the sailors, not expecting Jonah's response, were reticent to follow the instructions they were given. Jonah's instructions themselves raise several questions. How did he arrive at the conclusion that this was the proper course of action? Furthermore, why did the sailors need to throw him in? Why didn't Jonah just jump?

Jonah's suggestion may have been a matter of logic. Why was the storm sent? "To sink the ship" would have been a reasonable guess. What would sinking the ship accompliah for the LORD? It would punish Jonah. These may have been the thoughts that

passed through Jonah's mind. We wonder whether he was repentant. Perhaps he would rather die than carry out the commission given him by the LORD.

Why did Jonah force this action on the sailors rather than
jump overboard? It may be that he was simply too scared to
jump. On the other hand, the sailors had asked, "What shall we
do to you?" Perhaps Jonah's reply should be read more with the
tone of, "If you insist on doing something to me, throwing me
overboard will do the trick." Again, the text does not explain his
reasons, but as the episode unfolds, it becomes clear that even
this unusual course of action was used by the LORD to demonstrate His might to the sailors.

After the forementioned attempt to row back to shore, the
sailors resigned themselves to the fact that their only option was
to follow Jonah's instructions. Verse 14 shows that there was still
some concern on their part. Their request to Jonah's God as
phrased in the KJV and the NASB could be read two ways:

A. It could demonstrate their indecision. If he was guilty,
they did not want to die because of him. On the other hand, if he
was innocent, they did not want to be held responsible for shedding innocent blood.

B. It could demonstrate that their decision had been made,
but that they considered it a decision that they were not responsible for. In this case the two parts of the sentence are parallel:
"Do not let us perish for the life of this man, i.e., do not hold us
responsible for shedding innocent blood." They were not party
to his crime, and had no basis on which to judge his guilt or
innocence.

The NIV translates so as to favor option B, and this is indeed
the only way that the Hebrew can be read. The key phrase is
"for the life of" and 2 Samuel 14:7 shows that the phrase means
"for killing."

The sailors decided that they had to take Jonah's advice, but
they still seemed either unconvinced of his guilt, or unconvinced that his offense warranted such drastic punishment. In
effect, their action constituted what to them would appear to be

human sacrifice. Offended gods could usually be placated by additional sacrifices or libations, or perhaps by a larger donation of grain to the priests. Human sacrifice was not a normal practice in the Ancient Near East. It seems to have been resorted to occasionally, but was, for the most part, abhorrent.

The point that the sailors made was that the LORD had done as He pleased. That is, they were coerced into this course of action by the events that the LORD had brought about. The phrase also recognizes that God's ways are unfathomable (cf. Pss. 115:3; 135:6).

Having attached this disclaimer to their action, the sailors proceeded to carry out Jonah's instructions. In verse 4, the wind was "hurled" into the sea by the LORD. In verse 5, the cargo was "hurled" into the sea by the crew. In verse 15 Jonah was "hurled" into the sea as well.

The effect was stunning and, apparently, came about immediately. The sea stopped its raging. The beginning of verse 16 is identical in Hebrew to the beginning of verse 10, but this time the direct object "the LORD" is attached. In verse 10, the sailors were terrified. Jonah's revelation had them "scared stiff." The word translated "fear" in verse 10 is the same word that is used to describe awe or worship of a god. It is the same word used by Jonah in verse 9. In verse 16, then, the fear of the sailors had become a great reverential awe of the LORD. They sacrificed to Him (apparently after they had returned to shore) and made vows. What sort of vows would they have made? Most likely they were of a cultic nature. That is, they would have promised additional sacrifices, or the like. It must be kept in mind that both Canaanite and Mesopotamian religions understood cultic matters as being the sphere of the foremost demands of the gods. The performance of sacrifices and libations and the care of the temple were the primary religious responsibilities of the people. Even though the LORD was not like their gods, we would expect that they were not fully aware at this point of how much of a difference there was. While it is obvious that the calming of the sea would have had a lifelong effect on the sailors, the text gives no indication that it was a life-changing effect. No repentance is mentioned and there is certainly no indication that they renounced their other gods or converted to Judaism. Anyone who comes in contact with the power of the LORD cannot help but be awed by Him, but such awe does not necessarily produce a relationship with Him.

Meanwhile, Jonah found himself in an unusual, if not unique, situation.

C. The Great Fish (1:17)

> But the LORD ordained a great fish to swallow Jonah, and Jonah was in the inside of the fish three days and three nights.

This is, of course, the most well-known part of the book. In a way it is a shame that it has attracted so much attention, for in so doing, it distracts from the purpose and message of the book. The word that we have translated "ordained" demonstrates that this part of the book should be viewed no differently than the sprouting of the vine (4:6), the parasite that devoured the vine (4:7), or the east wind that tormented Jonah (4:8), for they were all similarly "ordained" by God.

The word itself has been translated several different ways (KJV: "prepared"; NASB: "appointed"; NIV: "provided"). Other uses of the word in this form occur in Job 7:3; Psalm 61:7 and Daniel 1:5, 10. The references from Job and Psalms are more useful for determining the meaning because God is the subject there as He is in Jonah. We feel that "ordain" is a more accurate translation. Besides fitting the contexts, it places the emphasis squarely on the sovereignty of God, the key issue behind the things that take place.

As has frequently been noted, the Hebrew speaks of a "great fish," not specifically a whale.[10] Discussion of gullet sizes of whales, sharks, etc., which species are native to the Mediterranean, and of case studies of sailors swallowed by fish and recovered alive are all of interest, but have no effect whatever on

[10]Similarly, the Greek of Matthew 12:40.

the text. The event is clearly portrayed in the account as a special act of God, and we would therefore not necessarily expect scientific corroboration that such an event is possible. Miracles are, by definition, impossible, or at least improbable, so the matter becomes only an issue of philosophy (i.e., are miracles possible), rather than an issue of scientific explanation (i.e., could this have happened). This will be discussed at greater length when the question of genre is addressed.

The length of time, three days and three nights, has been interpreted figuratively by some, but there is no example in the Old Testament in which three days can be shown to be a figurative representation.

Our first section has shown Jonah's unwillingness to embark on the mission that the LORD assigned to him. It has been made apparent, however, that as a prophet of the LORD, he had little choice in the matter. Other prophets were unwilling (e.g., Jeremiah, Moses), but none required coercion as did Jonah.

For Further Study

1. Have you been in situations where you were unwilling to follow God's instructions? How did you react? How should we react?

2. In a Bible dictionary or encyclopedia read articles on Jonah, Canaanite religion, Mesopotamian religion, and lots.

3. What did Jonah think he would accomplish by fleeing? Why did he not want to fulfill the mission?

Chapter 2

Jonah's Prayer and Deliverance
(Jonah 2:1–10)

We can imagine Jonah's life passing through his mind as those all-too-brief minutes elapsed and his lungs expended their supply of oxygen. With death imminent, did Jonah consider how he might have responded differently were he given a second chance? We really do not know.

Whether or not he saw the fish swimming toward him we are not told, but Jonah suddenly discovered that his environs had changed. The distastefulness of his temporary quarters would have been totally overshadowed by the sweet availability of oxygen. Jonah may or may not have known where he was, but he was happy to be alive. It is this sentiment that is expressed in the psalm of Jonah 2. There is no distress about having been swallowed by a fish, nor any question about what his fate would be, nor any prayer for deliverance from the fish.

We need not conjure up any image of Jonah like those in children's story books of Pinocchio and Geppetto sitting around a fire in the inside of the whale discussing plans for escape. Jonah is not sitting inside this fish with tablet and stylus in hand trying to compose poetic descriptions of his close encounter. His thoughts, as he perhaps drifts in and out of consciousness, are only of praise and thanksgiving that he has been miraculously spared. Most of the lines can be identified as standard poetic phraseology that is used in other Psalms as well (cf. Pss. 18:6; 42:7; and 69:1, 2, and 14 for a few examples).

And Jonah prayed to the LORD his God from inside the fish, and he said:

> I called to the LORD in my distress and He answered me.
> From the belly of Sheol I cried out; You heard my voice.
> You cast me into the deep, into the midst of the waters and currents surrounded me.
> All Your surf and waves passed over me.
> So I said to myself, I have been driven out of Your sight,
> Yet I will again gaze on Your holy temple.
> The waters encompassed me to the throat, the deep surrounded me,
> Seaweed was bound around my head.
> To the roots of the mountains I descended
> The underworld, its bars (closed) behind me forever,
> But You brought me up from the pit alive, O LORD, my God.
> As my life faded away, it was the LORD whom I thought of
> And my prayer came to You, to Your holy temple.
> Those who persist in empty vanities abandon their loyalty,
> But for my part, I will offer sacrifice to You with a voice of thanksgiving;
> That which I vowed I will fulfill;
> Rescue is from the LORD.
> Then the LORD spoke to the fish and it vomited Jonah onto the shore.

Jonah recalled crying out in distress to the LORD. He described himself as being in the "belly of Sheol" (KJV:Hell), thus drawing an interesting illustration: from the belly of Sheol to the belly of the fish. The word Sheol is of importance in formulating the Israelite philosophy of afterlife, so let us take a moment to examine it.

The term Sheol can be used in several different ways. Though the root meaning is disputed, it can be said with certainty that in Israelite thought the term referred to a place where the dead went (Isa. 14:9). It was considered to be under the earth (Amos 9:2). Those who were in Sheol were separated from God (Pss. 88:3, 10–12; 6:5–6; Isa. 38:18), yet God had access to Sheol (Ps. 139:8; Prov. 15:11; Amos 9:2). Sheol can be used as an expression for being close to death, or can be synonymous for the grave (Pss. 18:6; 30:3; 49:14; 116:3; Isa. 28:15, 18; Gen. 37:35; 42:38; 44:29, 31). It should be pointed out that the Old Testament nowhere states that everyone goes to Sheol. Psalm 9:17–18 can be read to imply that Sheol is not for everyone. More convincing, however, are the several passages that seem to present an alternative destination (Pss. 31:17; 49:15; 73:24; Prov. 14:32; 15:24; 23:14; Hos. 13:14). So far, the term is unattested outside of the Old Testament except for one occurrence in the Aramaic documents from the Jewish community at Elephantine (fifth century B.C.). We would conclude that Jonah used the term figuratively to describe the fact that he was at the brink of death.

Verse 3. Here the LORD is described as the one who cast Jonah into the sea. The waves are also described as belonging to the LORD, thus showing that Jonah fully realized that the sovereignty of God was in operation at every point of his ordeal.

Verse 4. Judging from the first part of the verse, Jonah is here still expecting death. This makes the assertion of the second part of the verse quite striking. While some have suggested a vowel change in the Hebrew to read the sentence: "How shall I look again on your holy temple?" we feel that such a change is unnecessary. Likewise we cannot agree with those who interpret Jonah's statement as anticipation of seeing the heavenly temple in the afterlife. Support for the latter idea is lacking in the Old Testament with the possible exception of the ambiguous evidence afforded by the passage about Ezekiel's temple (Ezek. 40–48). We would rather suggest that, as with verses 5–6, verses 3–4 tell of Jonah's past predicament and end with recognition that he had been rescued. Therefore he was cast out and driven away, but now he could again hope to have fellowship. This is parallel to verses 5–6 where he descended but was brought up.

Verse 5. Both KJV and NASB translate verse 5 similarly, speaking of water encompassing Jonah "to the very soul." The word used for soul however, has the physiological meaning of "throat" (Isa.

5:14; 29:8; 58:11; Prov. 3:22, parallel to "neck") which would seem to be more appropriate in this context.

Verse 6. The use of the figure of "the underworld (earth) with its bars" is used only here in the Old Testament. The sentence is difficult because it has no verb. The sense, however, would seem clear. The bars spoken of were the bolts on the gate to the underworld. Most city gates utilized bars for locking the gates. Akkadian literature attests the idea that the underworld has gates, specifically in the work called "The Descent of Ishtar." The word that we have translated as "underworld" in this verse is rendered in KJV, NASB, and NIV as "earth" and is the normal word for earth or land. Related terms in both Akkadian and Ugaritic are used for "earth" as well as "underworld."[1] The latter meaning may also be present in Old Testament passages such as Exodus 15:12; 1 Samuel 28:13; Job 10:21–22; Ecclesiastes 3:21; and Isaiah 26:19. This meaning however seems strongest here in Jonah where the parallel is the "roots of the mountains."

Verse 7. Just as Jonah was losing consciousness his thoughts focused on his God, and he prayed. He had remained loyal to the LORD to the very end (despite his disobedience): he had not turned to other gods.

Verse 8. The word translated "vanities" here is used other places in the Old Testament to refer to the worship of other gods (cf. Jer. 2:5; 10:3, 8, 15; 2 Kings 17:15). To turn to other gods, however, was to forsake the loyalty required by the LORD. Jonah vowed that he would offer a sacrifice of thanksgiving for the LORD'S rescue of him.

An important issue in this chapter is the question of whether or not this psalm implies that Jonah had repented and was now a willing prophet. Upon examination of the psalm, we do not find a single line that would suggest that Jonah had seen the error of his ways and was anxious to pack his bags and head for Nineveh. Furthermore, the attitude that he demonstrated in chapter 4

---

[1]Hebrew: *'eres;* Akkadian: *'erṣetu;* Ugaritic: *arṣ.* Cf. Nicholas Tromp, *Primitive Conceptions of Death and the Nether World in the Old Testament* (Rome: 1963), pp. 23ff.

suggests that the contrary was true. The lesson that Jonah seems to have learned was not that it was wrong to disobey the LORD and try to escape one's commission, but rather that it was fruit-less. Jonah, we would suggest, was not repentant, but was re-signed to the facts: He was going to Nineveh one way or the other. The LORD would not even allow Jonah's death to interfere with this mission. So while Jonah was clearly thankful that his life had been saved, the fact that no repentance is mentioned in chapter 2, and the persistence of his bad attitude in chapter 4, would indicate that this was the same Jonah who fled for Tar-shish. He had been shown that this was one job that he was not able to avoid.

The text does not state where Jonah was "dropped off" by the fish (which was, no doubt, very willing to jettison this unsavory piece of cargo). It would seem reasonable to assume, however, that Jonah was right back near Joppa where he started. The conductor is saying, "Let's try it from the top one more time." Reluctant obedience has instructive value, and Jonah was given the opportunity to demonstrate that he had at least learned this part of the lesson; so off he went to Nineveh.

For Further Study

1. In a Bible dictionary or encyclopedia look up Sheol.

2. Have you had an experience when you found that the Lord would not take no for an answer? What was the outcome?

3. What is the value of reluctant obedience for God? For us?

Chapter 3

Nineveh
(Jonah 3:1-10)

A. The City of Nineveh (3:1-3)

> Now the instructions of the LORD came to Jonah a second time saying: "Arise, go to that great city Nineveh and preach there the sermon which I speak to you." So Jonah arose and went to Nineveh in accordance with the instructions of the LORD (Now Nineveh was a great city to God; a three-day project).

There is, of course, a distinct contrast in Jonah's response this time. We are still not told the message that Jonah was to give, but we would not assume that the instructions were much different. Notice, however, that we have translated differently here than in 1:2. There our translation "denounce" represents the Hebrew phrase that approximates "call out against her." Here in verse 2 we translate the word as "preach." The Hebrew just uses a different preposition, "call out to her."

The trip between Joppa and Nineveh would have been between 500 and 600 miles, depending on the route that was taken. By camel or donkey caravan, it would have taken just under a month to traverse the distance. By foot it may have taken up to five weeks.

The parenthetical section of verse 3 gives us information about the task before Jonah. The city of Nineveh is described (in our translation) as "a great city to God." The reader will probably have already noticed that our translation differs from several major translations (KJV: "an exceeding great city"; NASB: "an ex-

ceedingly great city"; NIV: "a very large city").[1] These translations have rendered the word for God *('elohim)* as an adjective
meaning "mighty" or some other superlative. Other references
where this word is sometimes treated this way include Genesis
23:6 and 30:8. However legitimate that rendering may be in
these Genesis passages, Jonah 3:3 differs from them in that the
Hebrew here has a preposition before *'elohim*, thus putting it in
a totally different category. This usage has a parallel in Genesis
13:13 where the men of Sodom are described as "wicked men
and sinners to the LORD." Here the LORD is used rather than
God, so it could not possibly be an adjective or adverb, and the
preposition and syntax are similar to Jonah 3:3. It is unfortunate
that finding an example of parallel syntax does not always clarify
the meaning of the sentence. We have only been able to say
what it is not. By context we would suggest that this phrase
means "in God's estimation."

The city is further described as entailing a "three days' journey" (so KJV. NASB: "Three days' walk; NIV: "It took three days to
go all through it"). It is difficult to determine exactly what this
three days refers to. The city of Nineveh's most famous benefac-
tor was the Assyrian king, Sennacherib (704–681), who reigned
almost a century after the historical Jonah. In his own description of his building projects,[2] Sennacherib writes that he en-
larged the circumference of the city of Nineveh from 9300 cubits
(about 2-2/3 miles) to 21,815 cubits (about 6-1/4 miles). This
latter circumference is supported by archaeologists who meas-
ured the site at about 12km.[3] Obviously neither the circumlocution of the walls, nor a path through the diameter of the city
would constitute a three-day journey. Therefore several alternative solutions have been offered.[4]

D. J. Wiseman has suggested that "Nineveh" here is not just

---

[1]Both NASB and NIV, however, give translations similar to ours in footnotes.
[2]"A Palace Without Rival," see D. D. Luckenbill, *The Annals of Sennacherib.*
[3]Tariq Madhloum, "Excavations at Nineveh," *Sumer* 23 (1967), p. 77.
[4]Surveyed by D. J. Wiseman, "Jonah's Nineveh," TB 30 (1979), pp. 29–51.

ANCIENT
NINEVEH
(ADAPTED FROM ARCHAEOLOGIST
SKETCH, *SUMER* 23, 1967, p. 80)

Adad
Gate

Halahhigate

Nergal
Gate

Shibaniba
Gate

Sin
Gate

NINEVEH

Mušlal
Gate

Mashke
Gate

KUYUNJIK

Ninlil
Gate

Khosr River

Shamash
Gate

Tigris River

Madbari
Gate

NABI-
YUNIS

Handuri
Gate

Halzi
Gate

MODERN
MOSUL

Ashur
Gate

the city of Nineveh, but the administrative district which, he contends, may have included Assur, Kalah, and Dur-Sharruken. The circuit of these cities would have comprised about 55 miles, a long three days of walking (without much time for preaching).[5]

The NIV hints at another possibility when it translates the phrase "it took three days to go all through it." This would not be unreasonable. It should be remembered that the city gate was frequently the location of business transactions as well as of public proclamations or decrees. Sennacherib's Nineveh had more than a dozen gates around the city (see map of Nineveh). Jonah's itinerary would have included many, if not all of these gates, plus perhaps the palace, the temple courtyards, or other public places.

Further support of this interpretation of the three days is found in Nehemiah 2:6 where the king is trying to find out more about Nehemiah's proposed leave of absence. Concerning this passage, Wiseman himself notes:

> Artaxerxes would well know the distance and length of time needed to travel from Babylon to Palestine, a route, at least via Samaria, customarily taken by the mounted Persian postal courier service. His question concerned the length of Nehemiah's absence from his duties.[6]

So in the case of Jonah, we would interpret the comment not as a reference to the length of the journey, but rather as a comment on the size of the project. The task set before Jonah was expected to take him three days to complete.[7]

B. The Message of Jonah (3:4)

> And Jonah started to go through the city on the first day of the project preaching, "In just 40 days Nineveh will be overthrown!"

---

[5]Ibid., pp. 38–39.

[6]Ibid., p. 36.

[7]One final support for this is that when the Hebrew wants to describe a journey of three days, a different phrase is used (cf. Gen. 30:36; Exod. 3:18; 5:3; Num. 10:33).

This remains the only record we have of Jonah's message to the Ninevites. Was this all that he had to say? If he said more, why is only this line recorded? It seems unusual that the one proclamation that did not come to pass would be the only one that was recorded. Wouldn't the Ninevites have asked why this destruction was coming on them? Would not Jonah explain their wickedness and lead the way to repentance? In order to answer these questions, we must examine some aspects of religious belief in Nineveh and also take a closer look at Jonah's attitude.

Ninevite Beliefs. If someone were to come to your city and tell you that very shortly it would be destroyed, you would be full of questions. Who was going to do it? How? Why? What could be done to avoid it? How does the forecaster of doom know? The reaction of the ancient Ninevites would be quite different. The primary source of difference is in how Assyrians viewed their gods and understood the demands of their gods. Since they worshiped many gods, a single action could appease one god, but anger another. You could never tell what you may have done that would have been offensive. Certainly every god desired sacrifice, so failure to offer sacrifice to some god would be one possible offense. The requirements of the gods were primarily in the physical realm: sacrifices, libations, temple donations, and various cultic duties. Thus in their wisdom literature, we find sections like the following:

> Every day worship your god.
> Sacrifice and benediction are the proper accompaniment of incense.
> Present your free-will offering to your god,
> For this is proper toward the gods.
> Prayer, supplication and prostration
> Offer him daily, and *you will* get your reward.
> Then you will have full communion with your god.
> In your wisdom study the tablet.
> Reverence begets favor,
> Sacrifice prolongs life,
> And prayer atones for guilt.

He who fears the gods is not slighted by . [. .]
He who fears the Anunnaki extends [his days].[8]

Even of Shamash, the god of justice, it is said:

You observe, Shamash, prayer, supplication and benediction,
Obeisance, kneeling, ritual murmurs, and prostration.[9]

As a result, it is not uncommon in the literature that the individual feels he is being punished by the gods, but does not know why. A good example of this can be found in a piece entitled "A Prayer to Every God" found in the library of Ashurbanipal:

May the fury of my lord's heart be quieted toward me.
May the god who is not known be quieted toward me;
May the goddess who is not known be quieted toward me.
May the god whom I know or do not know be quieted toward me;
May the goddess whom I know or do not know be quieted toward me.
May the heart of my god be quieted toward me;
May the heart of my goddess be quieted toward me

. . . .
In ignorance I have eaten that forbidden of my god;
In ignorance I have set foot on that forbidden by my goddess.
O Lord, my transgressions are many; great are my sins.

. . . .
The transgression which I have committed, indeed I do not know;
The sin which I have done, indeed I do not know.
The forbidden thing which I have eaten, indeed I do not know;
The prohibited (place) on which I have set foot, indeed I do not know.
The lord in the anger of his heart looked at me;
The god in the rage of his heart confronted me;
When the goddess was angry with me, she made me become ill.
The god whom I know or do not know has oppressed me;
The goddess whom I know or do not know has placed suffering upon me.

---

[8]W. G. Lambert, BWL, 105:135–47.
[9]Ibid., 135:130–31.

Although I am constantly looking for help, no one takes me by
    the hand;
When I weep, they do not come to my side.
I utter laments, but no one hears me;
I am troubled; I am overwhelmed; I can not see.

. . . .

Man is dumb; he knows nothing;
Mankind, everyone that exists,—what does he know?
Whether he is committing sin or doing good, he does not even
    know.
O my lord, do not cast thy servant down;
He is plunged into the waters of a swamp; take him by the hand.
The sin which I have done, turn into goodness;
The transgression which I have committed, let the wind carry
    away;
My many misdeeds strip off like a garment.[10]

This differs from the case of Job, who knew that he had done
no wrong. His feeling of injustice came from the fact that he
knew the attributes and demands of his God. The Assyrians'
gods were capricious and unpredictable. As a result of this,
Ninevites would not necessarily ask why they were going to be
destroyed. Who could know the mind of the gods? One Babylonian penned the following:

I wish I knew that these things were pleasing to one's god!
What is proper to oneself is an offence to one's god,
What in one's own heart seems despicable is proper to one's god.
Who knows the will of the gods in heaven?
Who understands the plans of the underworld gods?
Where have mortals learnt the way of a god?[11]

Furthermore, even if the reason could be known, they would
not necessarily think that Jonah knew it. In Mesopotamia,
prophets were given messages of pending doom in dreams (for
the most part), and the reasons were not always given. Sometimes there was no reason. In the Lamentation over the fall of

---

[10]ANET, 391–392:1–7, 19–21, 26–38, 51–58.
[11]W. G. Lambert, BWL 41:33–38.

the city of Ur, Sin, the patron deity of the city asks why it was overthrown. The answer is given by Enlil, the head of the Pantheon:

> The verdict of the assembly cannot be turned back,
> The word commanded by Enlil knows no overturning,
> Ur was granted kingship, it was not granted an eternal reign,
> Since the days of yore when the land was founded to (now) when
>   the people have multiplied
> Who has (ever) seen a reign of kingship that is everlasting?[12]

Pronouncements of destruction could be made not only by prophets, but also by those who practiced divination, the reading of omens. It is likely that Jonah's pronouncement would have been verified by the omens before it was so totally accepted. Omens could be read from the movement of the heavenly bodies, from the actions of animals or the flight of birds, or from the configurations of the entrails of sacrificial animals.

All of the above deal with matters of paganism: omens and divination, capricious gods, and cultic rituals. The reader might object that while we are dealing with pagan Assyrians on the one hand, Jonah had come to Nineveh to represent the one God of Israel who is consistent and who requires moral behavior. Certainly this is true, yet Jonah was not sent, as far as we can tell, to preach the Israelite monotheistic religion to the Ninevites. We would contend, further, that Jonah was not even sent to preach repentance and that 3:4 does, after all, represent the full content of his message. This could be supported by several factors. First, we would expect that if only part of the message was recorded, it would be the most important part. Therefore, if Jonah had preached repentance, we would expect that to be preserved. While arguing that he did not preach repentance could be an argument from silence, arguing that he did has no evidence to support it. The actual repentance of the Ninevites is not evidence because, as we learn in 3:9, they did not know whether repentance would help or not.

---

[12]ANET, 617:366–70.

Another factor that leads us to expect that Jonah did not preach repentance was the attitude that prevailed in Jonah.

Jonah's Attitude. In our discussion of chapter 2, we suggested that while Jonah was thankful that his life had been spared, he was not necessarily contrite over his stubbornness. Chapter 4 will confirm that Jonah's attitude was still not what it should have been. How would this affect his preaching? Though we have not yet determined why Jonah was unwilling to go to Nineveh or why he did not want Nineveh to repent, we can assume that this attitude would make him very reticent to preach repentance if he did not have to. The last thing he wanted was for the Ninevites to escape their well-deserved doom.

In answer to our opening questions, then, we would suggest the following.

1. Jonah's message was one of approaching destruction—nothing else.
2. The Ninevites would not necessarily have pressed Jonah for more information because in their culture they would not assume that the prognosticator would have further information and, furthermore, would not necessarily have believed that reasons could be known. They would have assumed that his knowledge came from the some sort of omen. Omens give knowledge, not reasons.
3. Jonah's attitude was such that he certainly would not have offered more information than he was required to give.

It follows from this, and is born out in the text, that the Ninevites were not told that it was specifically the LORD, the God of Israel, who was going to bring this judgment on them, and neither did they express any belief in the LORD. This leads us to the next section.

C. The Response of Nineveh (3:5–10)

> And the men of Nineveh believed God, so they declared a fast and they dressed in sackcloth, from the greatest to the least of them. And the matter concerned the king of Nineveh and he

removed his robe and clothed himself in sackcloth and sat in dust. And he made a proclamation in Nineveh as follows: "The king and his court declare the following: 'Neither man nor beast, herd nor flock, shall taste of anything nor graze, nor shall they drink water, but they shall be covered with sackcloth, both man and beast, and they shall call sincerely to God. And let each man turn from his wicked way and from the injustice in which he's involved. Who knows but that the God may turn aside and relent from his burning anger and we will not be destroyed.'" And God saw their actions, that they did turn from their wicked ways, so God relented from the calamity which he intended to bring on them and he did not bring it.

Before we discuss the response itself, we might ask why these proud Ninevites would believe any Israelite. There are several things we should note in this regard.

First, as Wiseman points out, when delegations moved from country to country to conduct diplomatic affairs, it was not unusual for diviners or prognosticators to be part of the delegation, giving confirmation that the negotiations had the favor of the gods of the visiting delegation.[13] Kings were often interested in collecting all of the advice available in a given situation. There is an example of this in the Bible when Jehoshaphat asks to hear the advice of Ahab's prophets as they consider a joint military endeavor (1 Kings 22:2–7). This desire for advice from any quarter is especially true when something has happened that requires interpretation. Good examples can be found in the stories of both Joseph and Daniel who gave interpretations that had been revealed to them by God, but which were received by the foreign king like the results of any divination expert.

It is not impossible that Jonah's messsage was an interpretation of something that had recently occurred in Nineveh. Suggestions have ranged from eclipse, to earthquake, to invasion, but it need not have been anything that catastrophic. The reading of omens, as we have mentioned, was a practiced art in Assyria. It is possible that for days or weeks before Jonah's ap-

---

[13]D. J. Wiseman, TB 30 (1979), pp. 42–43.

pearance, all omens were predicting the downfall of the city. Such omens could involve the alignment of planets or stars within the zodiac:

> When the moon and sun are seen with one another on the fifteenth day, a powerful enemy will raise his weapons against the land. The enemy will destroy the gate of my city.[14]

They could likewise come from observation of animate or inanimate terrestrial occurrences:

> If ants are numerous at the entrance to the great gate; overthrow of the town.[15]

> If a fox runs into the public square, that town will be devastated.[16]

> If in some place there is an open well and bitumen appears, that land will be destroyed.[17]

Even the configuration of the liver or kidneys of sacrificial animals or the birth of malformed animals could signify devastating events to come. Even if Jonah's prediction was not the interpretation of omens that had been read prior to his arrival, it would be normal for the Assyrians to react to his message by checking the omens to see if they agreed.[18] It is therefore not difficult to accept the idea that the Ninevites would respond so amenably and readily to Jonah's preaching. His status as a foreigner would be no obstacle and his prognostication would have been double-

---

[14]R. C. Thompson, *Records of Magicians and Astrologers of Nineveh and Babylon* (London: 1900), #156.

[15]H. W. F. Saggs, *The Greatness that was Babylon* (New York: Hawthorn, 1962), p. 309.

[16]Ibid., 310.

[17]Ibid.

[18]Some have used the unusual coincidence that Jonah was coming from an experience with a fish, and that Nineveh itself was seemingly named after the goddess of fish, Nina (NANSHE) to suggest that Jonah's experience might have somehow served as a sign or omen to Nineveh. This is unlikely in that the omen literature was based on empirical observations, and it is not to be expected that the Ninevites had record of anything like what had happened to Jonah, so any such omen of this type would have no meaning to them.

checked. A greater problem arises in the nature of the Ninevite response to that message.

The response of Nineveh is first stated under the rubric "they believed God." NASB translates "believed *in* God," but in doing so a nuance is added that is not expressed in the Hebrew. If we compare Numbers 20:12, which uses the same Hebrew construction, it shows us that the phrase need not entail any more than believing what God had said. There is no indication in the Book of Jonah that the Ninevites turned from their other gods or made any sort of commitment to the LORD, or that they even knew the name of the LORD. The text only states that the message that Jonah brought from God was accepted as true.[19]

The first step taken by the Ninevites on hearing and accepting Jonah's message was the declaration of a fast and the donning of sackcloth. This was done by the people in verse 5 and was part of the king's decree in verses 7–8. Was this the normal way that Assyrians went about repenting? After examining Mesopotamian literature, we would have to come to the conclusion that this was very unusual behavior for Assyrians, or any other inhabitants of Mesopotamia. When faced with bad omens, misfortune, or other signals that a god had been offended, incantations were frequently resorted to to avoid the foretold consequences. Seeking forgiveness from one's god or goddess for wrongs or offenses (though unknown) would be another approach. The idea of repentance per se is difficult to pin down in Mesopotamian literature. When seeking the favor of a deity whose disfavor had become evident, however, sacrifices, libations, supplication and prostration were common actions. In a prayer to Sin, the moon god, after an eclipse, one worshiper recorded the following:

> I have spread out for thee a pure incense-offering of the night;
> I have poured out for thee the best sweet drink.

---

[19]Cf. R. E. Clements, "The Purpose of the Book of Jonah," VT Supp. 28 (1974), p. 18: "God's mercy which is extended to the people of Nineveh . . . is nowhere related to their embracing the torah, their rejection of idolatry, their acceptance of circumcision, nor even to so basic a feature as a confession that Yahweh the God of Israel is the only true God."

I am kneeling; I tarry (thus); I seek after thee.
Bring upon me wishes for well-being and justice.
May my god and my goddess, who for many days have been
angry with me,
In truth and justice be favorable to me;
May my road be propitious; may my path be straight.
After he has sent Zaqar, the god of dreams,
During the night may I hear the undoing of my sins;
Let my guilt be poured out.[20]

In another hymn to Ishtar, one of the primary Assyrian goddesses:

Ishtar, who but you can clear a path for him?
Hear his entreaties!
He has turned to you and seeks you.
Your servant who has sinned, have mercy on him!
He has bowed down and loudly implored you.
For the wrongs he committed he shouts a psalm of penance.[21]

The above examples are consistent with the rest of Mesopotamian literature that we have been able to check in that they lack any mention of fasting or sackcloth.[22] While fasting was not detectable in religious rituals, mourning rites, or for repentance in Mesopotamia, instances do occur when individuals refrained from eating and drinking. For example, there were special instructions for certain days throughout the Babylonian year. Catalogs were developed for lucky and unlucky days that listed what things were unlucky or forbidden on any given day.[23] In many of these, certain types of foods were taboo:

Onion he may not eat or a scorpion will sting him.[24]

---

[20]ANET, 386. Cf. also "A Prayer to Every God" quoted above.
[21]T. Jacobsen, *Treasures of Darkness* (New Haven: Yale University Press, 1976), p. 154.
[22]The translation "sackcloth" in ANET 384:60 cannot be maintained.
[23]S. Langdon, *Babylonian Menologies and Semitic Calendars* (Oxford: Oxford University Press, 1935).
[24]Ibid., p. 101.

Or:

> Fennel and watercress, cooked meat, and flesh of oxen, goats and swine, not to be eaten; all these rules, if broken, incur hatred ulcers and asthma.[25]

These could not be considered cases of fasting. However, in the instructions for the seventh day of the month of Tashritu, a late version says:

> One may not eat anything at all; it is an abomination to the god Urasha and the goddess Ningal.[26]

Other occasions when the Mesopotamians did not eat or drink seem to be similar to the situation recorded in Acts 23:12 when a group of men vowed not to eat or drink until they had killed the apostle Paul. One such text reads:

> By Bel and Nabu! When the messenger of my lord brought the message and delivered it, I did not take food or (even) water (until) I obtained X talents of iron and sent it to my lord.[27]

While these may be called fasting, there seem to be no spiritual or cultic connections to the act.

The nature of the Mesopotamian religion, furthermore, makes it very logical that the Ninevites would *not* have normally used fasting in a spiritual/religious sense. What, after all, is the purpose of fasting? Wherein lies its efficacy? Does God listen better to hungry people? The Israelites resorted to fasting for several different situations:

1. Mourning (1 Sam. 31:13; 2 Sam. 1:12; 1 Chron. 10:12; Ps. 35:13; Dan. 10:3).
2. Making Request to God (2 Sam. 12:16–23; 2 Chron. 20:3; Ezra 8:23; Neh. 1:4; Esth. 4:16; Jer. 14:12).
3. Sin (1 Sam. 7:6).
4. Official Fast Day (Jer. 36:1–10; Zech. 7:5; 8:19).

---

[25]Ibid., p. 101.
[26]Ibid., pp. 103–104.
[27]CAD L, p. 126.

5. Israelite Killed by Israelite(?) (Judg. 20:26; 1 Kings 21:9, 12).

Perhaps one of the most significant passages is Zechariah 7; for it gives us some insight into the reasons for fasting. While preparing to begin the last stage of rebuilding the temple, Zechariah was approached by a delegation and asked whether the people could now stop fasting on the day that commemorated the destruction of the temple. Zechariah replied with an answer that implies hypocrisy on the part of the people (vv. 5–6), and then proceeded to launch into a tirade on the failures of the generation that had been taken into exile and lectured them on morality. The connection was the issue of fasting.

The point so aptly made by Zechariah is still true today. The fasting for the temple was not a fast of mourning and sorrow over the temple, nor a fast to request its restoration, that it should cease when the temple was rebuilt. The fast was to be the result of the recognition that the people had strayed from their proper relationship with God. That was, after all, why God had allowed the temple to be destroyed. This was the purpose of Zechariah's preaching on morality. The concept behind this fasting was that individuals or groups became so distressed with their spiritual condition, or so aware of a need to make their relationships with God as close as it could possibly be, that the meeting of physical needs was, for the moment, the farthest thing from their minds. This is why fasting is tied to repentance. It also explains the connection between fasting and the efficacy of prayer. Proper fasting brings a person to the optimum point of fellowship and oneness with God, thus naturally increasing the efficacy of his prayers. Fasting is for personal revival.

Certainly Israel was not always aware of this ideal (see Isa. 58:3–6), but it was a concept that was within the range of the dynamics of their religious ideas. Such cannot be said for the Mesopotamian religion. We have already noted that the demands of the Mesopotamian gods were perceived by the people in terms of cultic caring for the gods (sacrifice, temple upkeep, etc.). The Mesopotamian gods did not demand nor model moral behavior or proper attitudes as did the God of Israel. We would be remiss, however, to imply that there was no ethical dimension to Mesopotamian religious practice.[28] The point is made by H. W. F. Saggs, however, that

> Some of the offences are plainly, from the modern point-of-view, ethical ones. The distinction between ethical sins and the unwitting breaking of taboos was however never clearly drawn, and was meaningless to the ancient Babylonian or Assyrian, who saw his religious duty in terms not of moral law but of the arbitrary and usually unpredictable will of a pantheon of gods.[29]

Ethical behavior (that is, action based on how one treats his fellow man) does not necessarily imply moral character (basing one's life on a consistent principle involving attitudes). The Mesopotamian gods were frequently ethical, but rarely even pretended to be moral. Shamash, as the god of Justice, was mainly responsible for insuring that justice was done in the world, i.e., for carrying out the retribution principle. Shamash never said "Do not use false weights for selling goods." He was merely praised for punishing those who did use false weights. Likewise he never dictated that his people should care for the widow or orphan; but his protection of those classes of people brought just rewards to those people who did so.

With all of this in mind, we are somewhat surprised to see the Ninevite reaction including fasting. The king's decree that called for the people to turn from their wicked ways was not out of line, for it involved primarily ethical reform. This is what we would expect from the Assyrians. Remember, they were not being converted to Judaism, the LORD, or even monotheism. This was purely a turning from wickedness. But if the Ninevite people were unaware of the LORD's demands on His people, Israel, and were unacquainted with a moral religious ideal, and showed no

---

[28]For examples: Hymn of Ninurta (BWL, p. 119); Hymn of Shamash (BWL, pp. 131–35); Hymn to Ishtar (ANET 384:40ff.; 385:80ff.); Hymn to Enlil (ANET 573:20ff.; 584:60ff.); Kramer, *Sumerians* (Chicago: University of Chicago Press, 1963); Hymn to Nanshe (pp. 124–25).

[29]Saggs, *The Greatness That Was Babylon*, pp. 306–307.

practice of religious/spiritual fasting, where did the idea of fasting come from? We cannot imagine that Jonah would have so instructed them. To an Israelite prophet the idea of fasting when no moral understanding or no relationship with the LORD was included would have been repulsive. There are four basic factors that would indicate that Jonah did not instruct the Ninevites to fast. First, the text reports nothing of such instruction on Jonah's part. Second, Jonah's attitude is such that we would not expect him to have volunteered such information. Third, the people's reaction shows no indication that they had any understanding of what they were doing. This would not likely be the case if Jonah had explained it to them. Finally, if Jonah had been telling them how to go about repenting, we would not necessarily expect fasting to head up the list of things that needed to be done. While none of these are conclusive in themselves, they all point to the probability that Jonah was not the source of the Ninevites' information on fasting.

If fasting was not a common practice for the Ninevites, and Jonah did not so instruct them, how can we account for their taking such a course of action? The answer is important for the rest of the story. It is likely that even though the Mesopotamians did not make use of ritual fasting, other peoples besides Israel did.[30] The priests, scribes, and specialists of Nineveh would have been able to discover (if not to discern) that Jonah was an Israelite, and it is not unlikely that they would have either had record of, or would have been able to find out who the Israelite God was and how his favor might be gained. This, combined with their probable awareness of the use of fasting among other peoples, would have dictated their official advice to the king. In this case, the efficacy of fasting most likely would have been perceived at best on an ethical level, or perhaps just for mourning.

In verse 6, the king left his throne. It is suggested by Wiseman that this action may indicate the performance of the *šar*

---

[30]There is mention of it in the Amarna letters (29:57).

puḫi ritual in which a substitute king was put on the throne to take the brunt of any misfortune foretold for the king.[31] The normal result for the substitute was death, so this amounted to human sacrifice. The occasion was frequently an eclipse of one of the major heavenly bodies. The ritual was replete with incantations and symbolic actions.[32] We see no evidence in Jonah to support the theory that this ritual was taking place. The king's coming off his throne was an act of humility, and of course, he had taken off his robe in order to clothe himself in sackcloth.

In verse 8, the animals were included in the order to don sackcloth. Many have noted that Herodotus IX, 24 has somewhat of a parallel when, to mourn the death of a Persian leader, the manes and tails of the horses were chopped short. This example would seem little different, however, from the modern-day use of a black hearse for bearing the coffin—even the vehicle denotes mourning. A nearer parallel to Jonah in ancient literature occurs in the apocryphal book of Judith (4:10–14) where animals were dressed in sackcloth as part of a day of repentance. It is possible, however, that this example derived from imitation of the Book of Jonah.

It is important to note that in verse 9, the Ninevites were uncertain whether their actions would cause God to set aside judgment or not. This is another indication that they were not receiving instructions from Jonah, and that repentance was not part of Jonah's message. If the message coming from the LORD specified repentance as an option, they would have had no doubt that their actions were sufficient to assure their safety.

The final result is stated in verse 10—God saw their actions and decided not to bring the judgment to pass. Again, it is evident that this was not a "saving faith" in that it was because of their actions that they were spared. It was not on the basis of any moral standard, nor for any faith; it was not due to any righteousness that they possessed. What actions or deeds are re-

[31]Wiseman, TB 30 (1979), p. 47.
[32]W. G. Lambert, "A Part of the Ritual for the Substitute King," *Archiv für Orientforschung* 18 (1957-8), pp. 109–12. No fasting is mentioned in this text.

ferred to? While the Book of Jonah is not explicit on this point, there are several other passages that mention the use of fasting and sackcloth that may be instructive.

In 1 Kings 21:27, Ahab and Jezebel had just brought about the murder of the innocent Naboth so they could lay claim to his vineyard. As a result of this, Elijah denounced Ahab and pronounced his doom (v. 21). Ahab's response was to put on sackcloth and fast (v. 27). The LORD in turn responded by *postponing* judgment because of Ahab's humility. It is of further interest that while Ahab's offense involved a moral wrong, it was in its most basic sense a breach of justice: an ethical offense.

A second example, Isaiah 58:3–6, likewise combines fasting and sackcloth, and humility again was stressed (vv. 3, 5). Furthermore, proper fasting was explicitly connected to ethical behavior (v. 6).

A final example not only connects fasting and sackcloth, but presents Israel in a situation similar to the one faced by Nineveh in the Book of Jonah. It is found in the Book of Joel. Here, the entire opening proclaims the approach of the Day of the LORD—a day of great judgment—just as Nineveh was warned of coming destruction by Jonah. Joel 1:13–15 mentions a response of fasting and putting on sackcloth (cf. 2:12). Further, Joel 2:14 repeats word for word the beginning of Jonah 3:9, and the end of Joel 2:13 is nearly identical to the last part of Jonah 4:2. Similarly, Joel 2:18 says that the Lord would spare His people, as He did with Nineveh. The significant difference is that the Ninevites turned from their wicked ways (Jonah 3:8), while in Joel, Israel was told "Return to me (the LORD) with all your heart" (2:12) and "Return to the LORD your God" (2:13). This was precisely the missing element for the Ninevites.

From the examples in 1 Kings 21 and Isaiah 58, we can deduce that the primary ingredient of the Ninevites' action was that they humbled themselves before God. As in the case of Ahab, and in contrast to the situation in Joel, this ethical response was sufficient for the LORD to relent from the precise judgment that He otherwise would have carried out.

For Further Study

1. In a Bible dictionary or encyclopedia look up: sackcloth, fasting, divination, Nineveh, and repentance.

2. What part does fasting have in Christianity today? What should occasion our fasting? What should characterize it?

3. Does it seem unusual to you that God would honor a repentance that was based on naïveté or ignorance? We would all agree that repentance is part of salvation, but does salvation always accompany repentance?

Chapter 4

Jonah's Lesson
(Jonah 4:1-11)

A. Jonah's Complaint (4:1-4)

> But to Jonah this was a great catastrophe and he was angry. So he prayed to the LORD as follows: "If You please, O LORD, was not this my complaint even when I was on my own soil? That was why I hoped to flee to Tarshish—because I know that You are a gracious and compassionate God, slow to anger and abounding in condescending love, to the end that You relent from bringing about calamity. And now, O LORD, please take my life from me, for I prefer dying to living." But the LORD said, "Do you have a right to be angry?"

What was it that had so distressed Jonah? One common suggestion is that he was angry at God for having spared the city. The difficulty of this suggestion is that judging from the end of 4:5, we are led to believe that Jonah did not know yet for a certainty that the LORD had relented. The statement in 3:10 was not made to Jonah, but was made for the reader's benefit. Furthermore, Jonah does not resent the fact that the LORD was characterized by the stated attributes. Knowing of these attributes, however, Jonah recognized that the response of the LORD would be in keeping with His character. The Ninevites had repented, so Jonah had no doubt that the LORD would relent. Was Jonah angry then that Nineveh repented? Many have suggested that as a good Israelite Jonah would have been delighted if Nineveh was destroyed. At the time of Jonah, however, Nineveh was not yet the capital city of Assyria and Assyria was not yet the world power that fifty years later would tyrannize Israel. Furthermore, their repentance would have been patently logical given the message that Jonah preached. Once doom had been pronounced and then confirmed by other means, the Ninevites would naturally seek to avert their destruction. Once Jonah presented his message, the rest of the results were practically inevitable: the people would repent, and the LORD would relent. He could not be distressed that they repented, for that was the only logical course of action.

What then was the source of Jonah's anger? I believe it was the entire chain of events. We have pointed out that it was all totally logical, and Jonah had foreseen it all from the moment of his call. This was why Jonah had fled, and he tells us as much. For Jonah, it was a no-win proposition from the start. He realized that if he went to Nineveh and pronounced their doom, the people would certainly make some attempt to appease the angry deity. But what did they know about the LORD and His demands? Their spiritual perception was extremely naïve, thus making it impossible that they could have any understanding of what they were doing. Yet Jonah knew that God, because of His attributes, would accept their shallow repentance anyway.[1]

Jonah was angry that the whole process was taking place. He would not be able to convert the Assyrians to a monotheistic belief in the LORD and had not been instructed to. But why should they be spared for such a superficial ritual, and for that matter, why should they even be warned? These questions deal with the purpose of the book and the lesson that God is teaching and will be discussed along with those matters in the next chapter.

Jonah demonstrated his insight both into the nature of God and into the nature of man. On the other hand it really rankled him that a more sophisticated understanding of moral law (or

---

[1]Cf. Millar Burrows, "The Literary Category of the Book of Jonah," *Translating and Understanding the Old Testament*, Frank & Reed (eds), (Nashville: Abingdon, 1970), p. 99, n. 19.

perhaps even of Jewish Torah) should not be required. This
interpretation of Jonah's anger is supported by the object lesson.

B. The Vine and the Parasite: The Object Lesson (4:5–8)

> But Jonah went out of the city and sat east of the city and made
> for himself a shelter, and sat under it in the shade until he could
> see what happened with the city. And the LORD God ordained a
> vine and it grew above Jonah to provide shade for his head to
> deliver him from his discomfort. And Jonah was very happy about
> the vine. But God ordained a parasite at dawn the next day and it
> attacked the vine so that it withered. And it so happened that
> when the sun rose, God ordained a scorching east wind and the
> sun beat down on Jonah's head, and he became dazed and he
> begged for death, saying, "I prefer dying to living."

The scientific identification of the particular vine[2] and parasite
that play their parts here is not possible, nor is it important for
the object lesson. The stress of the author is that God ordained
each in their role, just as He had ordained the great fish. There
is an important element, however, which is essential for the
interpretation of this passage, and which is not accessible to the
English reader. Perhaps the key to the object lesson is that the
word translated "calamity" in 3:10 is precisely the same noun
that in 4:6 is translated "discomfort." It is by this similarity that
we can make the correspondence which in turn lays open the
importance of the object lesson: *Jonah = Nineveh*. The people
of Nineveh were shielded from their *calamity* by their humility
and the ethical reform that had taken place. Jonah was likewise
shielded from his *discomfort* by the vine that grew up around
him.

It is also of interest to notice the switch that took place in this
section. Consistently throughout the Book of Jonah, Jonah spoke
to, and was spoken to, by the LORD, while the Ninevites referred
only to God. This is what we would expect, for the Ninevites
were threatened by "deity" whereas Jonah was in specific rela-

---

[2]For discussion, see R. K. Harrison, *Introduction to the Old Testament*
(Grand Rapids: Eerdmans, 1969), p. 910.

tion to his God, the LORD. In verse 6 of this chapter, at the beginning of the object lesson, the text states that "the LORD God ordained a vine . . ." and then proceeds, through verse 9, to use only the word "God" though He is dealing with Jonah. This is another indication that the object lesson is intended to somehow parallel the events at Nineveh. Just as it was "God" (as opposed to the designation the LORD) who was interacting with the Ninevites, so it was "God" who ordained the object lesson. Verse 6 perhaps uses both to signal the switch.

C. The Application (4:9–11)

> And God said to Jonah, "Do you have a right to be angry about the vine?" And he said, "I have a right to be angry unto death." And the LORD said, "You were concerned about the vine for which you did not work and which you did not cause to grow, which sprang up overnight and died overnight. So should not I, for my part, be concerned about the great city Nineveh in which there are 120,000 of mankind who do not know their right from their left, and a multitude of animals?"

In this application of the object lesson we find, as we would expect, God's answer to Jonah's complaint. In 4:4, God's question to Jonah about why he was angry went unanswered. Verse 5 led into the object lesson that was designed by God to help Jonah discover a different perspective on Nineveh's repentance (God's perspective), and in so doing would provide us with an answer to the question of 4:4. In regard to the event at Nineveh, Jonah was angry about the repentance of the Ninevites—not *that* they repented (for that was inevitable), nor that God should exercise His mercy (equally to be expected), but that such repentance (Jonah would hesitate to even call it that) should qualify for God's mercy. It just seemed unfair.

In the object lesson, the shoe was on the other foot. It was now Jonah who was the recipient (as was Nineveh) of undeserved grace. As before, Jonah's anger focused on the mechanism by which mercy was granted: here the vine, there the repentance. With Nineveh, however, Jonah was angry because the mechanism (repentance) worked, despite their ignorance about it. In the object lesson, Jonah was angry because the mechanism (the vine) failed to provide lasting results, though he likewise had no understanding of it.

In verse 9, God began to drive the point of the object lesson home. In verse 4 Jonah had been asked if he had a right to be angry about Nineveh. The question went unanswered. Now he was asked if he had any right to be angry about the vine. Jonah was quick to defend his right this time, and responded sharply with what was most likely a Hebrew expletive. Comparing the two situations, we find that Jonah's anger was very inconsistent. The mechanisms (repentance and the vine) functioned equally by the sovereign grace and mercy of God. Despite this, Jonah was angry that the mechanism in Nineveh's case worked, yet put in Nineveh's place, he was angry that it did not work. By this lesson, Jonah was shown that his anger about Nineveh had no real theological or philosophical base—rather, it was purely selfish. God had demonstrated that His mercy and grace do not function on the basis of merit, but are rather ordained by His sovereignty.

In verse 10, it was the LORD who again spoke (as opposed to "God"). He pointed out that Jonah was concerned about the vine, of which he had no understanding, and by that defended His (the LORD's) right in verse 11 to be concerned about Nineveh. This statement is the conclusion of the object lesson, and turns on the verb that we have translated "be concerned about" (cf. also NIV; KJV: "pity" or "spare;" NASB: "have compassion on"). The verb is used to characterize Jonah's attitude toward the vine and the LORD's attitude toward Nineveh. Though the same verb is used in both instances, it would probably be more accurate to translate it in different ways in that the object of Jonah's concern is inanimate. One does not have pity or compassion on a plant. The same verb is used with inanimate objects in Genesis 45:20 where Joseph instructs his brothers not to feel regret about leaving their possessions behind in Canaan. Obviously, they would not pity their possessions ("poor things have to stay in Canaan"), but rather might regret that they no longer have the use of them. Thus, the use of this verb with inanimate objects turns the attention on the subject. Jonah felt nothing for the plant itself, but regretted that it was no longer available for his benefit. The actual object of pity was himself.

When the verb is used with a person as the object, "pity" is a legitimate translation, but it must be understood to refer to a pity that is demonstrated by action on behalf of the one pitied. Therefore, by extension, "to spare" would be acceptable, for that is how God puts His pity into action.[3]

The force then of verses 10–11 is that just as Jonah regretted the failure of the plant and had pity on himself, so the LORD could defend His pity as a response toward the (feeble) repentance of the people of Nineveh. So again, *Jonah = Nineveh.* Nineveh was the object of the LORD's pity because of their repentance, and Jonah was the object of his own pity because of the vine.

Finally, the parallel was confirmed by the words the LORD spoke in verses 10–11. He noted that Jonah had no causal relationship to the vine at all. Jonah did not work for it, nor could he claim responsibility for it in any way. Parallel to this relationship between Jonah and the vine, the LORD characterized Nineveh as a city of 120,000 who did not know their right hand from their left. We believe that this could only refer to the moral naïveté of the Ninevites. Just as Jonah was shielded by the vine of which he had no understanding, and which he in no way deserved, likewise the Ninevites were shielded by a repentance that they neither understood nor deserved merit for. Jonah therefore was shown that he had no basis on which to begrudge the grace of God.

For Further Study

1. Do we sometimes let our preconceived notions or personal enmity create resentment toward what God is doing in the lives of others? How can we prevent these kinds of attitude problems?

---

[3]This verb is used opposite "destroy" in Ezekiel 20:17; 24:14.

2. What are some other examples in Scripture of God's mercy being extended toward the undeserving?

3. What obligation do we have to extend forgiveness to those whom God has forgiven? How can this principle be applied to situations that you face?

Chapter 5

Background of the Book of Jonah

A. Historical Background

Jonah. The only information about Jonah in the Old Testament outside of the Book of Jonah is found in 2 Kings 14:25. From this passage we can see that Jonah's ministry overlapped the reign of Jeroboam II. This places Jonah in the first half of the eighth century B.C. Jonah was from Gath-Hepher, a town in the Galilean region. As we see in 2 Kings 14, he prophesied to Israel, the northern kingdom. There is no indication whether he was a court prophet, such as Isaiah, or more of a renegade prophet, as Amos was.

The time period of Jonah's ministry may be very important to our understanding of the Book of Jonah. Prior to the time of Jonah, there were those familiar prophets such as Elijah and Elisha, and earlier still, Nathan and Samuel. Immediately subsequent to the time of Jonah, we enter the period of "classical prophecy" (primarily identified with the writing prophets, beginning with Hosea and Amos in the middle of the eighth century B.C.). There are several distinctions that can be made between classical and preclassical prophecy. One of the major ones is that the preclassical prophets addressed their messages primarily to the king, while the classical prophets addressed the people.[1] Jonah's role in the Book of Kings identifies him with the

---

[1]For discussion of this, see J. Holladay, "Assyrian Statecraft and the Prophets of Israel," HTR 63 (1970), pp. 29–51.

preclassical mold. The significance of this will be developed when we discuss the date and purpose of the book.

The time of Jeroboam II was a time of unparalleled prosperity for the northern kingdom of Israel. Assyria was in a stage of weakness and was preoccupied with her own internal security, and Egypt was still in decline. This left Jeroboam free to expand his borders, with the Arameans as the only hindrance. The Book of Jonah, however, speaks little of Israel, for Jonah's mission was to Nineveh.

Nineveh. Under Shalmaneser III in the middle of the ninth century B.C., the Assyrian Empire had had success in extending its control into the west, and had exercised its authority over Syria, Israel, Judah, and the many other western nations. The end of his reign, however, saw revolt by several Assyrian centers (including Nineveh). His son, Shamshi-Adad V, managed to subdue the rebellion, but during his reign, control over the west weakened considerably.

Shamshi-Adad V died about 811 B.C. and left as heir to the throne his young son, crowned Adad-Nirari III. Until the boy came of age the country was ruled by Shamshi-Adad's widow, Sammuramat, who seems to have retained extensive control until her death. Adad-Nirari reigned until 783 B.C. His city of residence and capital was Kalhu.

In seeking the identity of the Assyrian king connected with the Jonah story, Adad-Nirari has often been selected as a possibility because of an inscription of his that reads:

"In Nabu trust: trust in no other god."

This has been interpreted by some to imply that Adad-Nirari had monotheistic tendencies. While even a cursory reading of Adad-Nirari's inscriptions will show that such a suggestion has no evidence,[2] it should also be remembered that neither Jonah's message nor Nineveh's response had anything whatever to do

[2]D. D. Luckenbill, *Ancient Records of Assyria and Babylonia* (Chicago: University of Chicago Press, 1926), pp. 260–65. Adad-Nirari regularly invokes many Babylonian and Assyrian deities.

with monotheism. We therefore do not need to search for "monotheistic tendencies" in Assyrian kings when trying to date Jonah's mission.

Adad-Nirari III was succeeded by three of his sons, Shalmaneser IV, Assur-Dan III, and Assur Nirari V, respectively. This was a period of great Assyrian weakness, and in many respects could be characterized as practical anarchy. The Assyrians, Urartians, and Arameans occupied each other militarily while Israel and Judah expanded their boundaries to Solomonic dimensions.

All of this was reversed in 745 B.C. with the accession of Tiglath-Pileser III who, though he claimed kinship to Adad-Nirari III, began a new dynasty that established Assyrian supremacy for a century. Tiglath-Pileser III was succeeded by Sargon II, Shalmaneser V and, finally, Sennacherib, who was responsible for the enlargement of Nineveh. It was during his time that Nineveh became the capital of the Assyrian empire.

B. Date of the Book of Jonah

Let us first establish the boundaries within which the Book of Jonah must be dated. On the late end, the book must have been written prior to the second century B.C. This is ascertained by the fact that two apocryphal books thought to have been written during the second century B.C. demonstrate that they know of the Book of Jonah. Tobit 14:4, 18 mentions Jonah's exploits, while the Wisdom of Ben Sirach 49:10 speaks of "the twelve," showing that the canonical development of the twelve minor prophets had already been completed.

On the early end, we cannot, of course, go beyond the time in which Jonah lived. As has already been mentioned, Jonah's ministry fell within the confines of the first half of the eighth century B.C. It is difficult to be more specific because we do not know when the prophecy of 2 Kings 14:25 came in the reign of Jeroboam; we do not know whether Jonah's mission to Nineveh came before or after that prophecy; and we do not know how old Jonah was when either event took place.

Many conservative scholars still date the book to the lifetime of Jonah, but the consensus in recent years among scholars in general has been to date the book to the fourth or fifth centuries B.C. There are basically two objections raised to an early dating of the book:

1. The picture given of Nineveh is allegedly legendary and unrealistic.
2. The account is considered to be replete with "Aramaisms."[3] Let us take a closer look at these objections.

The Picture of Nineveh. There are three points in the claim that the picture of Nineveh is one of a past, legendary city, about which the details have become exaggerated with the passage of time. First, it is maintained that the size of the city is exaggerated ("a city of three-days journey, 3:3). Second, it is alleged that the account itself refers to the city as belonging to an age of the past ("Now Nineveh *was* a great city," 3:3, implying that it no longer is a great city). Finally, it is pointed out that the use of the title "King of Nineveh" shows an ignorance of truth in that neither biblical nor Assyrian sources ever refer to the king of Assyria as the king of Nineveh.

In the text analysis we discussed the phrase "a city of three-days journey" (which we translated "a three-day project") and so have already disqualified that objection. The phrase does not say anything about the dimensions of Nineveh, but rather addresses the time that it would take Jonah to complete his task. The observation that later Hellenistic sources attribute exaggerated proportions to Nineveh such that the circumference could be construed as requiring three days circumlocution is totally irrelevant.

The interpretation of the verb *was* as implying that the described condition no longer existed can simply not be grammatically supported. A few examples from biblical usage will suffice to demonstrate:

---

[3]"Aramaisms" are words that are common Aramaic words but have been adopted into Hebrew usage.

1 Kings 10:6—And she (the Queen of Sheba) said to the king (Solomon): "True indeed *was* the report which I heard in my land concerning you and your wisdom."

Isaiah 49:5c—"And I am honored in the eyes of the LORD and my God *is* my strength."

Jeremiah 14:4a (NASB)—"Because the ground is cracked, for there *has been* no rain in the land."

Though the English translations differ, the italicized word in each verse represents the same tense of the Hebrew verb "to be" as that used in Jonah 3:3, yet all clearly indicate continuing conditions. While it cannot be denied that the tense frequently refers to a past condition, these few examples show that it is haphazard to make absolute claims for the verb tense, and folly to use the tense of one such verb to date the book.

Finally, we must admit that the phrase "King of Nineveh" is enigmatic, but at the same time, it is rather intriguing. While, to be sure, the phrase is not used anywhere in Mesopotamian records, or even anywhere else in biblical records, neither have I seen it cited in any of the later Hellenistic writers. The argument, therefore, is not that the title is characteristic of late writing, but that it is unrealistic (because unattested). This then is an argument from silence. In reality, there are two additional ways in which the title could be explained:

1. It could be a legitimate, though unattested title of the king of Assyria;
2. It could refer to a ruler of the city of Nineveh, not the king of Assyria.

This first option presents several difficulties. Aside from the obvious fact that it is without supporting evidence, even the logic to support the possibility of such a title is questionable. Some have argued that since the Aramean king is called the king of Damascus, then it would be logical for the Assyrian king to be called the king of Nineveh. Though both are capital cities, the logic does not hold, for Damascus was a city-state while Nineveh was not.

The gravest problem with the king of Assyria being called the king of Nineveh is that during the time of Jonah, the king of Assyria did not have residence at Nineveh. Though Nineveh may have been a large and important city, it was not a royal city. During the time of Jonah, if any Assyrian city was to be part of a royal title, it would be Assur or Kalḫu, not Nineveh. Jonah would not have encountered the king of Assyria on his throne in Nineveh, because the king of Assyria did not have a throne in Nineveh.

The second option, that the "king of Nineveh" could have been the ruler of the city, has several good points, though positive evidence is still lacking. We have seen that during the lifetime of Jonah, the Assyrian empire was, for the most part, in a state of practical anarchy. A study of the inscriptions that were made by various provincial governors during this time supports this. The following summarizes the situation:

> The evidence seems to show that the governors of the western provinces displayed a tendency to independence during and after the reign of Adad-Nirari III. The reason may be that the central government with its control over federal administrators was weak; that the king was sustaining military defeats, and encouraged his governors to take the initiative at a time when Urartu was growing strong, infiltrating into contiguous countries and disrupting Assyria's trade routes.[4]

Is it possible that the governor of Nineveh had been granted this sort of independence or that the king's weakness had led Nineveh to establish some sort of independence? These are questions that cannot be answered on the basis of known data. This period in Assyrian history is very poorly attested.

Hebrew uses the term *melek* for king. The normal Akkadian (Assyrian) word for king is *šarru*, but there is a word related to the Hebrew *melek*, *malku*, which can be used to refer to kings or lesser officials. It is possible that the Hebrew term in Jonah 3,

---

[4]Stephanie Page, "The Stela of Adad-Nirari III and Nergal-Ereš from Tell al-Rimah," *Iraq* 30 (1968), p. 151.

melek, should be understood in terms of its Akkadian cognate, *malku*, but even this would not solve the problem entirely. The official in Jonah 3 would most likely be a governor. The term *malku* can refer to a governor, but the normal Akkadian title in such a case would be *šakinakku*.

While we are unable to explain the title "King of Nineveh," we have found that several explanations are possible, but all equally lack positive evidence. We must therefore, in good conscience, discard explanations of the title "King of Nineveh" as possible evidences for the date.

In summary then, none of the alleged evidences for the legendary or exaggerated picture of Nineveh can be maintained as a sound basis for objection to the early dating of the book.

Aramaisms. The term "Aramaism" refers to characteristically Aramaic elements (usually vocabulary) being used in the Hebrew text (having apparently been assimilated into Hebrew usage). Traditionally these Aramaic elements have been considered indications that the text was late. This is based on the presupposition that the elements were assimilated because of the status of Aramaic as the lingua franca (standard international trade language) of the Ancient Near East—a status that Aramaic supposedly did not achieve until the later periods, well after the time of Jonah. A more detailed discussion of this cannot be conducted here, but let it suffice to say that the nature of linguistic evidence and the ever expanding understanding of Northwest Semitic linguistic interchange warn against making conclusive chronological statements based on that sort of evidence.[5] The incident in which the Rab-shakeh (an Assyrian officer) is urged to use Aramaic in conversing with the inhabitants of Jerusalem in 701 B.C. (2 Kings 18:26) indicates that already at that time the use of Aramaic was dominant. There is therefore little basis for denying the possibility of Aramaic influence even in the time of Jonah.

---

[5]For some additional, though not overly technical discussion of the Aramaisms, see Leslie Allen, *Joel, Obadiah, Jonah and Micah* (Grand Rapids: Eerdmans, 1976), p. 187.

We might note at this point that the question of whether Jonah was written in the eighth century B.C. or in the fourth century B.C. has no effect on the question of whether the events recorded in the book actually occurred. A fourth-century date of writing would not preclude an accurate account of facts from the eighth century having been passed down orally. This makes the issue of Aramaisms even less significant. On the other hand, even if it could be established that the book was written in the eighth century, we would still not have absolute proof of its historicity. In short, we need to keep in mind that the date that the book was written is inconclusive for determining historical accuracy.

If the details about Nineveh and the Aramaisms do not help us to date the book, what other criteria might be used? We would suggest that a more profitable area for examination would be in the development of the prophetic institution in Israel. If we could identify Jonah with a certain stage within the development of prophetic thought in Israel and could, by such an identification, explain to some extent Jonah's strange behavior, we may have some clues for dating the book.

We have already mentioned that one of the distinctions between the preclassical and classical prophets was that the former had addressed (primarily) the court, while the latter focused their attention on the people. Another change that seems to occur with the advent of classical prophecy is in the area of repentance. Y. Kaufmann observes that

> The earliest biblical stories give no place to repentance. The generations of the flood and the tower of Babel, the men of Sodom, and the Canaanites are not called upon to repent. Nor does Moses avert God's wrath from Israel by rousing them to repentance; he intercedes on their behalf, invoking God's promise to the patriarchs and the glory of his name (Ex. 32:11ff.; Num. 14:13ff.; Dt. 9:26ff.).[6]

We might add that there is likewise no mention of repentance by individuals such as Adam, Cain, and Achan. As a prophet,

---

[6]Y. Kaufmann, *Religion of Israel* (New York: Schocken, 1972), p. 284.

Elijah, like Moses, interceded but did not ask the people for repentance, only commitment (2 Kings 18:21, 37).

There is other evidence, however, which leads us to modify somewhat the statement made by Kaufmann. In 1 Samuel 7:3, Samuel does call on the people to repent. Samuel, of course, is not a good example of a preclassical prophet, because prior to the accession of Saul, there was no "court" for him to address. His relationship with the people combined his roles as prophet, priest, and judge. Though Samuel may be only an exception, we feel that all we have evidence to say is that the *task* of the preclassical prophet was not that of leading people to repentance, nor of pronouncing doom. This is not to say that he never engaged in these things. This was simply not the nature of God's messages to man until we get to the period of classical prophecy. Certainly we can see that Amos can be characterized in the classical mold of pronouncing doom, calling for repentance and, at times, suggesting some cause for hope.

Can we identify precisely when this shift took place? Do the historical books take note of the change? J. Holladay suggests that we can, and that this theological development took place not only during the lifetime of Jonah, but that it can be connected with the ministry of Jonah.[7] In 2 Kings 14:25 Jonah prophesied that the border of Israel would be restored to Davidic dimensions. This prediction flies in the face of the statement of the previous verse, which identified Jeroboam II as "evil in the sight of the LORD." The editor justifies the anomaly in verse 27 by saying that the Lord had not yet threatened punishment. No prophet had been sent to warn the people of coming destruction nor, seemingly, to urge them to repentance.

Just a few chapters and some fifty years later, the assertion is made that "The LORD had warned Israel and Judah through all his prophets and every seer saying 'Turn from your evil ways and keep my commandments, my statutes according to all the law

---

[7] J. Holladay, "Assyrian Statecraft and the Prophets of Israel," HTR 63 (1970), pp. 47f.

which I commanded your fathers, and which I sent to you through My servants the prophets'" (2 Kings 17:13 NASB).

We again can see clearly that Jonah fits into the preclassical category of prophets. He did not preach repentance to either Israel or Nineveh. However, while the situation in 2 Kings 14:25 is very suitable to preclassical prophecy (i.e., the king is addressed, and the people are held unaccountable), Nineveh's repentance is strikingly unusual. It is this dichotomy, however, that suggests an explanation of Jonah's attitude toward his mission.

We have previously suggested that Jonah was angry because he saw the whole situation as a no-win proposition. This was connected to the fact that given Jonah's message, the Ninevites would seek to appease the Israelite God, yet could not possibly understand His demands. Could it be, however, that Jonah's attitude was also a reaction against what he saw as a change in divine policy? Why was Nineveh being warned? After all, had Sodom been warned? It is the warning that made naïve repentance possible. Why tell them at all? He certainly did not intend to intervene on their behalf.

Jonah thus can be seen to bridge the gap between preclassical and classical prophecy. His attitude and frame of mind were that of a preclassical prophet, but he was commissioned to the job of the classical prophet. The shift appeared to baffle him.

On the basis of this analysis, we would identify the Book of Jonah as the product of at least the preexilic period, for it rightly preserves the tensions that existed in the eighth century B.C. The author of the Book of Kings likewise demonstrates knowledge of the tension between preclassical and classical prophecy, but we would not necessarily expect this to be preserved in Jonah if the book was a product of the postexilic period. Certainly we can verify that the *events* of the book are proper to the background of the eighth century B.C.

C. Author of the Book of Jonah

There is no reason to deny Jonah authorship. However, there is no reason to assume that this biographical sketch must be autobiographical. We agree that some of this must have derived from Jonah, but there is no biblical evidence.

D. Purpose of the Book of Jonah

The purpose, as we interpret it, focuses on the changes brought about by classical prophecy. The example of Nineveh is intended to educate both Israel and her prophets in regard to what might be called the "ground rules" of the new era. It is the mechanism by which the age of classical prophecy is introduced. Through Amos, Hosea, Isaiah, Jeremiah, etc., Israel and Judah were going to be warned of coming judgment. This was going to come in the form of prophetic pronouncement—usually deemed irrevocable. The Book of Jonah tells them that repentance was a proper and acceptable response, and could even turn back the pronouncement of the prophet (which, of course, was the pronouncement of the Lord). It had worked even for Nineveh, a naïve, wicked, pagan city (cf. Ezek. 18:21). When the warnings came to Israel (2 Kings 14:27 tells us they had not yet), here was the example. Even though doom had been pronounced, repentance could bring mercy.[8]

The choice of Nineveh as the example was not really unusual. Though Assyria was in a period of decline at the time of Jonah, and Nineveh was not the capital city, by the time the lesson was to become pertinent, things had turned around and both were in the limelight.

The identification of the above purpose does not, of course, imply that there are no other lessons taught in the book. We would continue to maintain, for instance, that the tension of naïve repentance vs. informed monotheism is a point on which the author intends to instruct Israel. We do, however, reject the current interpretation that the Book of Jonah was written to scold Jewish exclusivism in the postexilic period. This view assumes that Jonah was asked to preach repentance and does so.

---

[8]Though arrived at independently, a similar understanding was expressed by R. E. Clements, "The Purpose of the Book of Jonah," VT Supp. 28 (1974), pp. 16–28.

We find no evidence for such an assumption in the book. Furthermore, such a purpose has not been convincingly integrated with the object lesson of chapter 4.[9]

It likewise seems unnecessary to try to explain Jonah's negative attitude as patriotism or concern for his prophetic reputation. The former position argues that Jonah would have been anxious for Assyrians to be destroyed on political grounds. As we have seen, however, at the time of Jonah, Assyria was not an oppressor of Israel. On the contrary, Assyria frequently tended to aid Israel indirectly by keeping the Arameans occupied.

Concerning Jonah's prophetic reputation, we can see that he might have been concerned that something that he had prophesied was not coming to pass, but it is difficult to derive from that concern a purpose for the book that is consistent with the object lesson of chapter 4.

While our interpretation of the purpose and date understands the Book of Jonah as less symbolical and puts it closer to the time of Jonah, it still does not necessarily prove that the events of the book are historical. Determination of historicity comes under the discussion of genre.

E. Genre of the Book of Jonah

It is of the utmost importance to make one thing very clear at the beginning of this section. It is not our intent to enter into a debate of whether or not the events recounted in the Book of Jonah *could* have happened. C. S. Lewis has aptly pointed out that in discussion of a miracle that someone has claimed took place, the issue cannot center on whether such an event is *probable;* for its classification as a miracle clearly characterizes the event as most highly improbable. Thus, an event that is miraculous should not be dealt with only in terms of historical or scientific probability. It is a philosophical issue.

We begin then with the philosophical belief that miracles *can* occur. Therefore, we have no difficulty in accepting as miracles

---

[9]For discussion of the weakness of this interpretation and others, see Clements, Ibid.

several events in the Book of Jonah. If these be miracles, it is useless to discuss the gullet sizes and geographical habitats of dozens of species of whales, or the chemical content of mammalian digestive juices and their projected effect on human epidermis over prolonged periods. If we wanted to discuss this sort of thing, we would have to begin with first things first and ask whether or not God could talk to man (Jonah 1:1).

Once given the philosophical presupposition that miracles can occur, our task becomes a literary one, for we must determine whether the author intended to claim that miracles *did* occur. This is now no longer a philosophical or theological discussion. Granted that God can direct a large fish to swallow a man and drop him off three days later, we must ask whether the author is actually claiming that God *did* do that to Jonah, or whether He wants to make a point by telling us a nice little story that He never intended us to accept as historical event. Certainly God *could* make a talking lion to rule a world such as Lewis portrays Aslan in the *Tales of Narnia*, but Lewis does not claim that God *did*, so it would be silly to argue the historicity of Narnia.

Our literary task, then is to determine, if possible, the genre of the Book of Jonah. What type of literature is it? What was the author attempting to do? What claims are made, directly or indirectly, by the book?

The claims of the book are not forthright. The author never makes the outright declaration that the things written were actual events. This makes us dependent on the form and style that were used. Are there indications in how the book was written that the author intended to convey actual events? We might better ask, are there any indications that he did not so intend? To answer this question, we must examine some of the alternatives that have been suggested for the genre of Jonah.

Earlier this century it was popular to interpret Jonah as an allegory. The word "Jonah" means dove, and it was claimed that the dove was a symbol of Israel. Therefore, Jonah was seen to represent Israel, while the fish supposedly represented Babylon who "swallowed" Israel (the captivity) as a punishment for her refusal to carry out her missionary mandate to the gentile world (Nineveh). Some even went so far as to identify the vine of chapter 4 with Zerubbabel. Several problems can immediately be detected in such an interpretation:

1. The identification of Israel with a dove can in no way be considered standard or common.
2. Babylon is never mentioned, and Babylon took only Judah captive, not Israel (remember, Jonah was of the northern kingdom, Israel).
3. In the Book of Jonah, the fish is clearly a means of deliverance, not of punishment.
4. The Exile is not brought on Judah for failure to carry its religion to the Gentiles, but for failure to keep themselves free from the influence of other religions.
5. Jonah's message had nothing to do with the propagation of Judaism, Torah, or monotheism, therefore eliminating any missionary aspect of Jonah's task.

Today it is not uncommon for established conservative scholars to present Jonah as a parable. Among more liberal scholars, it is the only alternative, having replaced the untenable allegorical interpretation presented above. The primary characteristic of a parable is that it has a moral or didactic aim. It must certainly be admitted, however, that a historical story can likewise have a "moral or didactic aim." The Books of Kings were not recorded simply because they were history, but because of the lessons that were taught. How then, we might ask, could a parable be differentiated from a historical story with a lesson? The only way is if some hint is given that the events told did not really occur. This could be done by the teller in many various ways. A characteristic of the parables of Jesus is that in telling them He does not use names and does not set them in a chronological framework. In Jonah, these indicators are divided. The historical name of Jonah is used, but no time frame is given ("In the third year of Jeroboam, king of Israel, the word of the LORD came to Jonah . . . ," or something along that line is what we would have hoped for in order to identify the intention as clearly historical), and the name of the Assyrian king (or Ninevite governor) is not mentioned.

While the absence of a time frame could be used to support a theory that the book of Jonah is a parable, we feel that that is insufficient in and of itself. We would therefore conclude that the book should be taken historically, as we have treated it throughout this commentary. The linguistic and conceptual elements as well as historical information all support its authenticity.

In regard to the genre then, our position on the Book of Jonah can be summarized as follows:

1. Unless we would rule out the possibility of miracles (and we do not), we have no reason to doubt that the events took place.

2. We have no compelling reason to insist on the story being a parable, and therefore we affirm its historicity.

This discussion has been based on the evidence available in the book itself. Many would claim that we also must be guided by the information afforded by the New Testament references to the Book of Jonah. We would agree that this information need also be taken into account, but feel that as a general rule it is profitable to keep Old Testament and New Testament data distinct in the process of the evaluation. Having now completed our analysis of the Old Testament data, we turn to the New Testament.

F. The Sign of Jonah

Many have felt that Christ's use of the example of Jonah constitutes evidence for the historicity of the events. Therefore, in conclusion, we would like to address that issue. Three passages comprise the references of Christ to the "sign of Jonah:" Matthew 12:39–41; 16:4; and Luke 11:29–32. The context of the sayings is the request of the Pharisees for a "sign," presumably to authenticate Christ's message. In response to this request, the Pharisees were told they would get no sign but the sign of Jonah. In Matthew 12 Christ proceeded to make the analogy that as Jonah was three days in the belly of the great fish, so the Son of man would be three days in the earth. In both Matthew 12 and Luke 11, Christ comments that the Ninevites would stand up at judgment and condemn the Pharisees for their unbelief. Neither the analogy of Matthew 12, nor the future act of the Ninevites are positively identified as the "sign of Jonah" that had been mentioned. Luke 11:30 gives the only positive clue: "For just as Jonah became a sign to the Ninevites, so shall the Son of man be to this generation." We must ask then, how Jonah "became a sign to the Ninevites." While it is possible that Jonah's experience with the fish was used by him as a sign to the Ninevites, the text of Jonah makes no such connection. If this connection is not made in the text, we cannot expect that Jesus would have assumed that His questioners would know what He meant by the sign of Jonah. There is nothing in the rabbinic traditions to indicate an interpretation that Jonah used the fish incident to authenticate his message.

We feel that it is best to understand the words for exactly what they say: Jonah himself became the sign. The Pharisees were asking for a sign so that they might have confirmation of the message Jesus was giving. It will be remembered that we suggested that the Ninevites would have sought similar confirmation of Jonah's message, or, more likely, that all the omens for weeks (months?) had pointed toward the overthrow that Jonah predicted. In this case, Jonah became a sign to the Ninevites by the timing of his visit. He came and preached a message that perhaps in itself was a verification of the signs that had been read in the omens by the Ninevites. While this is not specified in the text of Jonah, it does seem to be one of the few options that fit the statement of Luke 11:30. Further confirmation can be found in Matthew 16:1-4. There the mention of the sign of Jonah is in the context of Jesus' criticism that the Pharisees can discern the signs of the weather, but "cannot discern the signs of the times." The time was ripe for the Messiah. Jesus' appearance and message were confirmation of the other signs, as Jonah's message confirmed (by our suggestion) the Ninevites' signs.

However the sign of Jonah may be identified, we must still deal with the effect of the comments of Jesus on the historicity of the Book of Jonah. The question we are dealing with is, "Could the analogy drawn by Jesus in Matthew 12:40 be based on a literary reality rather than a historical reality?" I have encountered no conclusive evidence for either a positive or negative answer to that question, and therefore feel that the case for historicity must not be made on this issue. There is another factor, however, that is often overlooked. In both Matthew 12:41 and Luke 11:32 Jesus mentions the Ninevites standing up in judgment and condemning the Pharisees. It would seem much more difficult to understand this as a literary reference, for it is clear that Jesus considered "judgment" to be an event that would actually occur. Further, from these verses, we see that He expected the Ninevites of the Jonah account to be there. This surely must lead to the conclusion that Jesus believed that the repentance of the Ninevites in response to the preaching of Jonah actually occurred. This, in turn, rules out the possibility that He was treating the book as literary composition only. It is this point that serves as evidence for the claim that Jesus considered the Book of Jonah to be historical and so ought we.

G. Lessons From the Book of Jonah

It has often been noted that the Book of Jonah teaches obedience to the command of the Lord. That is certainly true, but we should not stop there. Jonah learned the hard way that in some matters, the choice is not whether to obey or disobey; rather it is whether we yield to God's command or leave Him no choice but to drag us. There are times when God will not be denied—we can go willingly, grudgingly, or by pure force, but *go* we will.

Another lesson learned by Jonah was that nice, neat theological categories do not confine God. God is not limited to our perception or understanding of Him. This is not to say that there are no theological absolutes. Jonah found, however, that there were fewer than he thought.

Finally, in connection with both of the above, we see in Jonah a spiritual pride that we should all strive to avoid. Jonah felt that he knew best how God works, and even disregarded God's attempts to lead him out of his misconceived presuppositions. Our job is to do, not to understand, the directions of God as He guides our lives and our ministries.

For Further Study

1. Look up in a Bible encyclopedia or dictionary: Assyria, Aramaic, parable, allegory, Jonah (Book of), and Jeroboam II.

2. In what guises does spiritual pride show itself in our lives?

Bibliography

Aalders, G. Ch. *The Problem of the Book of Jonah*. London: Tyndale Press, 1958.

Allen, Leslie. *Joel, Obadiah, Jonah, and Micah*. Grand Rapids: Eerdmans, 1976.

Archer, Gleason. *A Survey of Old Testament Introduction*. Chicago: Moody, 1974, pp. 307–15.

Bewer, Julius. *A Critical and Exegetical Commentary on Jonah*. Edinburgh: T & T Clark, 1912.

Childs. B. S. "The Canonical Shape of the Book of Jonah," in *Biblical and Near Eastern Studies*, pp. 122–28. Edited by Gary Tuttle. Grand Rapids: Eerdmans, 1978.

Clements, R. E. "The Purpose of the Book of Jonah," *Vetus Testamentum Supplement* 28 (1974), pp. 16–28.

Freeman, Hobart E. *An Introduction to the Old Testament Prophets*. Chicago: Moody, 1968, pp. 160–71.

Haran, Menahem. "The Rise and Decline of the Empire of Jeroboam Ben Joash," *Vetus Testamentum* 17 (1967), pp. 266–97.

Harrison, R. K. *Introduction to the Old Testament*. Grand Rapids: Eerdmans, 1969, pp. 904–18.

Haupt, Paul. "Jonah's Whale," *Proceedings of the American Philosophical Society* 46 (1907), pp. 151–64.

Holladay, John. "Assyrian Statecraft and the Prophets of Israel," *Harvard Theological Review* 63 (1970), pp. 29–51.

Kaufmann, Yehezkel. *The Religion of Israel.* New York: Schocken, 1972, pp. 282ff.

Keil, C. F. *Minor Prophets.* Grand Rapids: Eerdmans, 1973 reprint.

Laetsch, Th. *The Minor Prophets.* St. Louis: Concordia, 1956.

Pfeiffer, Robert. *Introduction to the Old Testament.* New York: Harper, 1948, pp. 586–89.

Scott, R. B. Y. "The Sign of Jonah," *Interpretation* 19 (1965), pp. 16–25.

Wiseman, D. J. "Jonah's Nineveh," *Tyndale Bulletin* 30 (1979), pp. 29–51.